THE
BATTLE
OF BRITAIN

THE BATTLE OF BRITAIN

Summersdale Publishers Ltd
46 West Street
Chichester
West Sussex
PO19 1RP
UK

www.summersdale.com

Printed and bound in the Czech Republic

ISBN: 978-1-84953-742-1

Substantial discounts on bulk quantities of Summersdale books are available to corporations, professional associations and other organisations. For details contact Nicky Douglas by telephone: +44 (0) 1243 756902, fax: +44 (0) 1243 786300 or email: nicky@summersdale.com.

THE
BATTLE
OF BRITAIN

A MISCELLANY

NORMAN FERGUSON

summersdale

Contents

Introduction

*Who the hell were these chaps to come over
into our sky and drop bombs on us?*
RAF Squadron Leader Douglas Bader

The Battle of Britain was the first major battle to be
fought solely in the air and it was the only battle of the
Second World War to be fought in plain view of the
British population.

The Battle of Britain's significance is still subject
to debate: did it stop Hitler from invading? Was it a
foregone conclusion that the superior strength of the
Royal Navy would halt any cross-Channel incursion?
Was the battle really decisive?

While it is subject to mythologising, there can be no
doubt that the German armed forces – which did not
suffer a reverse up until the autumn of 1940 – were
not victorious. The expected defeat of Britain's air
force did not materialise. Britain was left to fight on in
the war.

DATES

The official British dates of the battle are 10 July to 31 October 1940. Air fighting had taken place before and continued after, but commander of RAF Fighter Command, Air Chief Marshal Hugh Dowding, decided on 10 July as being the start of the battle as it was the first time the Luftwaffe sent large formations to challenge Fighter Command, although, as he wrote, 'operations merged into one another almost insensibly'.

AUTHOR'S NOTE

Dates given are for 1940 unless otherwise indicated.

Timeline

1935

NOVEMBER

6   The Hurricane makes its first flight.

1936

MARCH

5   The Spitfire makes its first flight.

JULY

14   Air Chief Marshal Dowding is appointed head of Fighter Command.

1938

AUGUST

4   19 Squadron receives the RAF's first Spitfires.

1939

SEPTEMBER

3   Britain and France declare war on Germany.

OCTOBER

16   First German air raid on Britain. Two Junkers Ju 88s are shot down by Spitfires.

1940

APRIL

9   Germany invades Norway and Denmark.

MAY

10   Germany invades France and the Low Countries.

10   Winston Churchill becomes British Prime Minister.

14	Rotterdam is bombed; 814 civilians are killed.
14	RAF bombers lose 40 out of the 71 that attack German forces near Sedan in northern France.
15	Dutch forces surrender.
15	RAF launches its first large-scale raid as 99 bombers attack the Ruhr.
21	For the first time, Hitler discusses invasion of Great Britain.
26	Operation *Dynamo*, the evacuation of Allied troops from Dunkirk, begins.
27	Belgian army surrenders.

June

4	Dunkirk evacuation ends.
5/6	Small-scale bombing of Britain begins with raids on targets in the south-east and east coast of England.
5	RAF Coastal Command begins invasion patrols over French ports.
10	Norway surrenders.
18	Last RAF aircraft return to bases in Britain from France.
18	In a speech to Parliament, Churchill declares that the Battle of Britain is about to begin.

22   France signs Armistice with Germany.

27/28 Liverpool, Newcastle and Southampton are
       bombed.

30   Göring issues directive on the air war against
       Britain.

JULY

2   Despite reservations, Hitler orders invasion
      preparations to begin.

3   RAF Bomber Command begins attacking
      invasion barges.

10   Channel battle begins as Luftwaffe attacks
      British shipping and ports.

16   Hitler issues Directive Number 16, preparing
      for *Unternehmen Seelöwe* (Operation Sea Lion).

19   Hitler makes peace offer to Britain.

21   Hitler determines invasion must take place by
      15 September.

21/22 First successful use of Airborne Interception
      radar by RAF as a Blenheim shoots down a
      Dornier 17.

AUGUST

1   Hitler issues Directive Number 17 directing the
      Luftwaffe to destroy the RAF.

13   *Adlertag* (Eagle Day). Luftwaffe launches large-
     scale raids on RAF radar stations and airfields.
15   All three Luftflotten (air fleets) attack targets
     around Britain.
18   Luftwaffe fly almost 1,000 sorties and suffer
     heavy losses on 'The Hardest Day'.
18   Last use of Ju 87 Stukas in large-scale operations.
19   11 Group commander Keith Park orders
     his squadrons to defend the sector stations, to
     operate only over land and to target bombers.
20   Churchill speaks in Parliament praising 'the Few'.
24   Luftwaffe bombs central London for the first
     time.
25   RAF bombs Berlin.

SEPTEMBER

7   Luftwaffe raids on London during the day and
     night mark the beginning of the Blitz.
7   Fears spread when a code word is
     misinterpreted, indicating the invasion is taking
     place.
11   Hitler postpones making a decision on invasion
     until 14 September.
14   Hitler postpones decision on invasion until
     17 September.

15   Luftwaffe launches what they hope will be a decisive major attack on London.

17   Hitler postpones invasion indefinitely.

OCTOBER

12   Hitler orders preparations for invasion to continue, in order to keep the pressure on Britain.

31   Official end of the battle.

1941

MAY

10   The Blitz ends with a raid on London that kills 1,436 people.

JUNE

22   Germany invades the Soviet Union.

1942

FEBRUARY

13   Hitler finally orders all remaining Sea Lion invasion forces to be deployed elsewhere.

People of the Battle

THE COMMANDERS

BRITAIN

PRIME MINISTER WINSTON CHURCHILL

Churchill became Prime Minister the same day as Germany invaded France and the Low Countries. He defiantly pursued a course of keeping Britain in the war, while others considered suing for peace. Churchill's leadership during the battles of France and Britain is regarded as one of the crucial elements in ensuring eventual victory for the Allies.

88 PER CENT

Churchill's approval rating in July 1940, as reported in a Gallup poll.

AIR CHIEF MARSHAL HUGH DOWDING

I was fighting the Germans and the French and the cabinet and the Air Ministry and now and again the Navy for good measure.

Known as 'Stuffy' because of his reserved manner, the ex-First World War pilot was responsible for the system providing the aerial defence of Britain. Although respected and admired by those who served under him, he did not set out to win friends in the political world of the senior echelons of the RAF and government. Despite being due to retire, the manner of his leaving his command in November 1940 was felt by many to lack respect for his achievements.

AIR VICE-MARSHAL KEITH PARK

If ever any one man won the Battle of Britain, he did.
Marshal of the RAF Lord Tedder, on Park

Experienced in both the combat and administration aspects of the RAF, Park was much respected by his subordinates. Despite his successful leadership of

11 Group – the most challenged group in the battle – Park was posted to Training Command following the battle.

OK I

Code painted on Park's personal aircraft, a Hurricane, in which he toured the airfields under his command to motivate his personnel and get a first-hand perspective.

AIR VICE-MARSHAL TRAFFORD LEIGH-MALLORY

12 Group commander Leigh-Mallory disagreed with Park and Dowding over tactics and replaced Park as commander of 11 Group in December 1940. He commanded Allied air forces during the Normandy landings of 1944 and was flying to a new appointment as head of South-East Asia Command in November 1944 when his plane crashed. He was the highest-ranked RAF officer to die in the war.

GERMANY

REICHSMARSCHALL HERMANN GÖRING

Göring, who shot down 22 Allied aircraft in the First World War, was an early supporter of Hitler and secured senior positions in the Nazi hierarchy, including head of the Luftwaffe. He amassed great wealth through bribery and the misappropriation of artworks and was fond of personal shows of ostentation – he had flamboyant uniforms made for himself and his main mode of transportation was a personal train.

DER DICKE (THE FAT ONE)

Luftwaffe crews' nickname for Göring.

GENERALFELDMARSCHALL ALBERT KESSELRING

Nicknamed 'Smiling Albert', Kesselring was an effective and able leader. He commanded Luftflotte 1 in the invasion of Poland and, following the Battle of Britain, led Luftflotte 2 during the invasion of the Soviet Union. He was later overall German commander in the Mediterranean theatre, where he again faced Keith Park, who was by then in charge of the island's Allied air defences.

GENERALFELDMARSCHALL HUGO SPERRLE

As commander of Luftflotte 3, Sperrle was under no illusions about the strength of RAF Fighter Command during the Battle of Britain. He later commanded the Luftwaffe in North Africa, where his aircraft supported Rommel's Afrika Korps, before being given charge of the German air forces which faced the Allied invasion of Normandy in 1944.

THE PILOTS

RAF

FLIGHT SERGEANT JAMES 'GINGER' LACEY

With 501 Squadron, Yorkshireman Lacey flew in the Battle of France, where he made his first kills, shooting down four aircraft. In the Battle of Britain he shot down 18 aircraft, becoming the highest-scoring British pilot.

SQUADRON LEADER ADOLPH 'SAILOR' MALAN

If you shoot them down they don't get back and no one in Germany is a wit the wiser. So I figure the right thing to do is to let them get back. With a dead rear gunner, a dead navigator, and the pilot coughing his lungs up as he lands... I think if you do that it has a better effect on their morale.

Called 'Sailor' because of his time in the Merchant Navy, Malan was one of the RAF's many Commonwealth pilots. As commander of 74 Squadron he was keen to dispense advice to protect his pilots and improve their offensive abilities. Fellow fighter pilot Al Deere described him as 'the best fighter tactician and leader produced by the RAF in World War Two'. In peacetime he campaigned against apartheid in his homeland of South Africa.

250 YARDS

Malan, along with some other pilots, had his machine guns set to reach a point 250 yards in front of his aircraft, rather than the prescribed 400 yards. The 0.303-inch calibre bullets were not as effective in damaging enemy aircraft unless fired as close as possible.

SQUADRON LEADER DOUGLAS BADER

Bader had lost both legs in an aircraft accident in 1931 but regained his RAF flying certification in 1939. A determined and outspoken commander, he was shot down over France in 1941 and taken prisoner, ending up at the prisoner-of-war camp in Colditz Castle, Germany. His life was portrayed in the book and film *Reach for the Sky*.

LUFTWAFFE

MAJOR ADOLF GALLAND

Like his rival Werner Mölders, with whom he vied to become the highest-scoring Luftwaffe fighter pilot, Galland had flown in the Spanish Civil War. During the Battle of Britain he commanded III/JG26, a Jagdgeschwader (fighter wing) with a reputation for combat prowess. The flamboyant Galland, whose fighter's cockpit had a cigar lighter installed, was given a senior command in August 1940 during a period when Göring replaced many of the older commanders with younger blood. He ended the war with 104 victories, 3 more than Mölders.

'BALE OUT, YOU BED-WETTER!'

Exasperated instruction by Galland to a nervous pilot asking for guidance during a dogfight.

OBERST WERNER MÖLDERS

Nicknamed '*Vati*' ('Daddy'), Mölders played an important role in the development of Luftwaffe tactics. He survived a dogfight with Malan's 74 Squadron on 28 July 1940 and went on to shoot down 50 aircraft by October. He was killed in an aircraft accident in 1941.

The Aircraft

RAF

Fighters

Vickers-Supermarine Spitfire Ia

The Spitfire was an aeroplane beyond all compare.
Wing Commander Robert Stanford Tuck

Maximum speed: 354 mph at 18,500 feet
Maximum altitude: 34,700 feet
Climb speed: 5.4 minutes to 15,000 feet;
                            7.7 minutes to 20,000 feet
Range: 575 miles (maximum); 395
                            miles (with 15 minutes
                            combat)
Armament: 8 x 0.303-inch machine guns

Number built:	1,583 Mark Is; 920 Mark IIs; 20,334 total for all marks
Crew:	1
First flight:	5 March 1936
Entered service:	4 August 1938

Vickers-Supermarine produced seaplanes and flying boats and had won three consecutive Schneider Cups (air race time trials) between 1927 and 1931 with designs created by chief designer R. J. Mitchell. His first attempt at a monoplane fighter was a failure and was abandoned, but the next design proved to be much more successful: the Spitfire was the only Allied fighter to remain in production throughout the war and it remained in RAF service until the 1950s.

SHREW

Name preferred by Mitchell for the aircraft. When he heard it was to be called Spitfire, he said, 'It's just the sort of bloody silly name they would choose.'

£4,500

Price for each Spitfire in the first contract issued by the Air Ministry on 3 June 1936. The initial order was for 310 aircraft.

GERMAN INFLUENCE

The Spitfire's construction was influenced by a German aircraft, the Heinkel He 70. The Spitfire's wing designer Beverley Shenstone had been impressed by the Heinkel's smooth surfaces, which were achieved by using countersunk rivets.

VISIBILITY

The Spitfire's long nose obstructed pilots' front vision when they were on the ground, so they had to taxi in a zigzag pattern. When landing, they flew a curved approach to ensure the runway was kept visible for as long as possible.

CANNON SPITFIRES

In June 1940, Spitfires fitted with two 20-mm cannon instead of their normal eight machine guns were delivered to 19 Squadron. This operational trial was not a huge success: the guns frequently jammed and the squadron asked to have their old aircraft back.

SPITFIRE VERSUS ME 109

The two aircraft were closely matched and at times it was down to the pilots' abilities who would win a dogfight. The Spitfire was slightly faster below 15,000 feet, and slightly slower above 20,000 feet. It had superior manoeuvring and turning circle at all altitudes, but the

Messerschmitt could outclimb and outdive it. Towards the end of the battle the improved-performance Mark II Spitfire came into service and gave its pilots the edge.

Spitfire snobbery

Term coined by RAF pilot Peter Townsend to describe the Luftwaffe crews' claims of always being shot down by Spitfires, and not Hurricanes, despite the majority being shot down by Hurricanes.

'A squadron of Spitfires!'
Adolf Galland's reply on being asked by Göring
what he required to win the battle.

Hawker Hurricane I

*She was solid… steady as a rock – a
wonderful gun platform.*
Wing Commander Robert Stanford Tuck

Maximum speed:	316 mph at 20,000 feet
Maximum altitude:	33,750 feet
Climb rate:	5.9 minutes to 15,000 feet;
	8.4 minutes to 20,000 feet
Range:	680 miles
Armament:	8 x 0.303-inch machine guns
Number built:	3,857 Mark I; 14,533 built
	for all marks

Crew:	1
First flight:	6 November 1935
Entered service:	25 December 1937

The Hurricane was the RAF's first monoplane single-seat fighter, developed from designer Sydney Camm's own Hawker Fury biplane design. Hawker was so confident of its potential that preparations began for its construction before any official order had been placed.

It brought new features to the RAF, such as a retractable undercarriage and an enclosed cockpit, although its fuselage was covered in fabric, rather than the stressed metal skin of the Spitfire – but this also meant Hurricanes were quicker to manufacture, so at the beginning of the war there were double the number of RAF Hurricane squadrons compared to Spitfires.

'A PIECE OF CAKE'

Description of flying the Hurricane by test pilot George Bulman after its first flight. It was more docile to handle than a Spitfire.

FUEL TANK

One of the drawbacks of the Hurricane's design was the reserve fuel tank, which was located in front of the pilot. When hit, it caused the pilot to become engulfed immediately in flames, leaving him with little time to escape.

Hurricane versus Me 109

The Hurricane was slower and was outdived and outclimbed at all altitudes by the German fighter, but it had better manoeuvrability at low level and could out-turn the Me 109 at any height. It could also absorb heavier punishment from enemy fire and rough handling by inexperienced pilots.

Spitfire and Hurricane

The Battle of Britain could have been won by the Spitfire but had we not had the Spitfire the Hurricane could not have won it on its own.
Alex Henshaw, Spitfire test pilot

Wheel track

Much was made of the difference between the planes' respective wheel tracks – the distance between the main wheels. A narrower track led to greater instability when landing or taxying.

Hurricane	7 feet 7 inches (2.3 m)
Spitfire	5 feet 8½ inches (1.7 m)

You could taxi as fast you liked, the undercarriage was as strong as the Forth Bridge.
'Ginger' Lacey on the Hurricane

15 SECONDS

Firing duration of both planes' eight machine guns. Each aircraft carried 2,400 rounds of ammunition.

30 MPH

Speed lost by the machine guns' recoil.

AMMUNITION

The machine guns fitted to both aircraft used the same 0.303-inch calibre bullets as the Lee Enfield rifles used by the infantry. The bullets came in three different types:

Ball
Armour-piercing
De Wilde explosive-incendiary

The De Wilde bullets were popular because their impact was visible to the pilots, serving as an aiming aid.

ROLLS-ROYCE MERLIN

Both aircraft were powered by one of Britain's most famous engines: the Rolls-Royce Merlin. The version of the V12 engine fitted to most of the machines in the battle could produce 1,310 hp (with boost). Merlins were later used in legendary aircraft such as the Lancaster and the Mosquito, and over 168,000 were made by the time production ended in 1951.

CONSTANT SPEED

Early Spitfires and Hurricanes were fitted with propellers which were either fixed in pitch – the angle at which the blades cut through the air – or which could be set to two settings: one for take-off (fine pitch) and the other (coarse pitch) for the rest of the time in the air. When new variable-pitch, constant-speed propellers were brought in through a rapid programme of work, there was an immediate increase in aircraft performance.

BOULTON PAUL DEFIANT

The Defiant... should prove a very sharp
thorn in the side of the raiding Germans.
Flight, 9 May 1940

Maximum speed:	304 mph at 16,500 feet
Maximum altitude:	30,000 feet
Climb rate:	8.5 minutes to 15,750 feet;
	10.2 minutes to 18,000 feet
Range:	465 miles (at cruising speed);
	600 miles (maximum)
Armament:	4 Browning 0.303-inch
	machine guns (in turret)
Number built:	1,064
Crew:	2
First flight:	11 August 1937
Entered service:	December 1939

The Defiant's only armament was four machine guns mounted in a rotating turret operated by a gunner, situated behind the pilot. It was intended to be used against unescorted bombers, the rationale being that German fighters would not have the range to reach Britain (it had been assumed leading up to the war that France would not fall in any conflict).

In the Battle of France, Defiants had found success. German pilots mistook them for Hurricanes and were surprised by their rearward-firing guns, but they soon found a weakness: Defiants were extremely vulnerable to head-on attacks where the turret could not be aimed effectively.

590 POUNDS

Weight of Defiant's gun turret.

141 & 264

These squadrons were equipped with Defiants at the beginning of the battle. Following heavy losses, they were taken out of front-line day service and converted to become night fighters.

LUFTWAFFE

BOMBERS

JUNKERS JU 87B 'STUKA'

Maximum speed:	232 mph at 13,500 feet (cruising speed 175 mph at 15,000 feet)
Maximum altitude:	24,500 feet
Range:	370 miles (with 1,100 pounds); 875 miles (with fuel tanks only)
Armament:	3 x machine guns (2 in wings, 1 in rear cockpit)
Bomb load:	1,100-pound bomb or 1 x 550-pound bomb and 4 x 110-pound bombs. Could carry 2,200-pound bomb for short missions.
Number built:	5,709 (total for all marks)
Crew:	2
First flight:	Spring 1935
Entered service:	June 1937

Like several other Luftwaffe types the Ju 87 first saw action in the Spanish Civil War. It was an effective ground-attack aircraft, particularly in the blitzkriegs in Poland and western Europe.

Each Stuka had two sirens fitted on the front of their wings, to add to the psychological effect of their dive-bombing. However, at the bottom of the dive, slow and low, they were vulnerable to attack. They suffered heavy losses in the early part of the battle and were pulled out of action in mid August.

STURZKAMPFFLUGZEUG

Generic term for a dive-bomber which when shortened became the common name for the Ju 87: Stuka.

KESTREL

Like the Me 109, the Ju 87 first flew with this British Rolls-Royce engine.

13,000 FEET

Typical altitude at which the Stukas began their dives. They dived at 300 mph and bombs were released at around 2,000 feet.

'STUKA PARTY'

Name RAF pilots used for occasions when they were able to inflict heavy losses on the slow and lightly armed dive-bombers.

JUNKERS JU 88A-1

Maximum speed:	286 mph at 16,000 feet
Maximum altitude:	26,500 feet
Range:	1,553 miles
Armament:	Up to 8 machine guns (in cockpit nose and rear, and in ventral gondola)
Bomb load:	5,500 pounds (maximum); 3,968 pounds (normal)
Number built:	15,100 (total for all marks)
Crew:	4
First flight:	December 1936
Entered service:	September 1939

The early Ju 88s were fast but following the success of the Ju 87, Ernst Udet, in charge of Luftwaffe aircraft procurement, insisted on the new bomber being able to dive-bomb. The imposed changes added to its weight as the fuselage was strengthened and heavy dive brakes added.

The Ju 88 was insufficiently armed and its crews were not protected by enough armour. It still remained the most capable of the German bombers and was later used in a number of roles, including as a successful night fighter.

25,000

Number of changes made to the Ju 88 during its development.

FIRST DOWNED

The first German aircraft to be shot down over Britain were Ju 88s. On 16 October 1939, as they bombed Royal Navy warships in the Firth of Forth, nine were attacked and two were shot down by Spitfires of 602 and 603 Squadrons.

DORNIER DO 17Z-2

Maximum speed:	265 mph (at 16,400 feet)
Maximum altitude:	26,740 feet
Range:	745 miles
Armament:	Up to 8 machine guns (in cockpit nose, side and rear, and in ventral gondola)
Bomb load:	2,205 pounds
Number built:	535 (total for all marks)
Crew:	4
First flight:	23 November 1934
Entered service:	Early 1937

The Dornier was reliable but slower than the Junkers Ju 88 and could carry less of a bomb load than the Heinkel He 111.

'THE FLYING PENCIL' ('DER FLIEGENDER BLEISTIFT')

Nickname given to early Do 17s because of their thin fuselages.

5K + AR

Fuselage code of Dornier Do 17Z-2 recovered from the Goodwin Sands, Kent, in 2013. It had been shot down on 26 August 1940. After over 70 years in the sea the tyres of the main undercarriage were still inflated. 5K + AR – the only surviving example of the type – was taken to RAF Cosford for preservation.

HEINKEL HE 111-H

Maximum speed:	255 mph at 16,000 feet
Maximum altitude:	25,500 feet
Range:	1,212 miles (maximum); 760 miles (with full bomb load)
Armament:	Up to 8 machine guns (in cockpit nose, side fuselage, dorsal gondola and ventral gondola)
Bomb load:	4,400 pounds
Number built:	5,600
Crew:	5/6
First flight:	24 February 1935
Entered service:	1937

In its heyday the Heinkel was fast and it was thought that it wouldn't need much defensive armament, as it would be able to outrun any pursuing fighters. This no longer applied by the start of the battle and it suffered against RAF fighters. Adding guns and armour only made it heavier and slower.

600 POUNDS

Weight of armour plating (but with their large Perspex canopies, Heinkel 111s were vulnerable to frontal attack).

'*STERBEBETT*'

Crews' nickname for the under-fuselage gun position. It translates as 'death bed'.

75 PER CENT

Percentage of Luftwaffe bomb tonnage dropped during the Blitz by He 111s.

LUFTWAFFE

FIGHTERS

MESSERSCHMITT ME 109E-3

Maximum speed:	354 mph (at 12,300 feet)
Maximum altitude:	34,450 feet
Climb rate:	6.2 minutes to 16,500 feet
Range:	412 miles (without combat)
Armament:	2 cannon (wings); 2 machine guns (nose-mounted)
Bomb load:	550-pound bomb or 4 x 110-pound bombs (E-1B and E-4B marks)

Number built:	1,256 (E-3); 34,000 (total built, all marks)
Crew:	1
First flight:	28 May 1935
Entered service:	February 1937

The Me 109 was Germany's only single-seat fighter of the battle. Luftwaffe pilots were anxious about the aircraft's wing strength and were wary of turning too tightly in case it led to structural failure. The Me 109 was powered by a Daimler-Benz 601 engine which had better performance than the Merlin at high altitude.

7 SECONDS

Duration of Me 109 cannon fire.

60 SECONDS

Duration of Me 109 machine-gun fire.

20 MINUTES

Length of time an Me 109 could spend over south-east England. Flying in combat or weaving to keep station with bomber formations reduced their endurance. Despite an extra fuel tank being available for the later E7 variant, it was not used as pilots were worried it would explode if hit in combat.

MESSERSCHMITT ME 110 C-4

Maximum speed:	340 mph at 22,000 feet
Maximum altitude:	32,000 feet
Climb rate:	8.5 minutes to 18,000 feet
Range:	565 miles (high-speed cruise)
Armament:	2 x 20-mm cannon,
	4 machine guns (nose);
	1 machine gun (rearward firing)
Bomb load:	1,100 pounds
Number built:	6,050 (all marks)
Crew:	2
First flight:	12 May 1936
Entered service:	1937

This twin-engine, well-armed Messerschmitt was designed as a *Zerstörer* (Destroyer) – a heavy fighter intended to be a long-range bomber escort. It was not very manoeuvrable, suffered heavy losses and itself had to be escorted by Me 109s. It was later used as a successful night fighter.

RAID 42

In May 1941, a single Me 110 was tracked and designated by radar stations as 'Raid 42' as it flew in from the North Sea over Northumberland and into Scotland. The aircraft was flown by Hitler's deputy, Rudolf Hess, who had embarked on an unauthorised solo peace mission. Hess parachuted to the ground and after his venture failed, spent the rest of his life in prison, dying in 1987 at the age of 93.

THE PLANE THAT NEVER WAS: HEINKEL HE 113

Despite not being in service, RAF pilots sometimes reported shooting them down. Heinkel had produced a prototype fighter called the He 100, which was depicted in propaganda photographs as 'He 113', but which never in fact made it into production. In the heat of battle, aircraft recognition was not always accurate and, in addition to the misidentification of enemy aeroplanes, 'friendly fire' incidents were not uncommon.

AIRCRAFT PRODUCTION

While the capability of RAF squadron pilots to fly and fight effectively was vital, another important element was the supply of fighters.

MINISTER FOR AIRCRAFT PRODUCTION

Soon after Churchill became Prime Minister on 10 May he appointed his friend, the newspaper owner Lord Beaverbrook, as the government minister responsible for aircraft production. Beaverbrook brought determination and ruthlessness to the job, although part of his success was due to improvements in production (e.g. the use of subcontractors) that had been put in place before his appointment.

0

Number of Spitfires built at Birmingham's Castle Bromwich factory by May 1940. The running of the plant was taken by Beaverbrook from Lord Nuffield (who had manufactured Morris cars) and given to Vickers-Supermarine, who brought in their own staff to reorganise production. The plant went on to make almost half of all Spitfires made.

FIGHTER PRODUCTION

German intelligence underestimated the RAF's strength and British industry's ability to resupply. As the Luftwaffe was prepared for a short aerial offensive, not a long-term war of attrition, it did not have the same reserves available to it.

Single-seat Fighter Production			
MONTHS (1940)	ME 109	SPITFIRE	HURRICANE
June	164	103	309
July	220	160	272
August	173	163	251
September	218	156	252
October	144	149	250
TOTAL	919	731	1,334

LOSSES AND PRODUCTION

During the battle, the RAF began to lose aircraft at a higher rate than the Luftwaffe, but Britain's aircraft production and repair capability was better.

RAF OPERATIONAL FIGHTERS

MONTH	DAY	NUMBER
July	13th	666
	20th	658
	27th	651
August	3rd	708
	10th	749
	17th	704
	24th	758
	31st	764

September	7th	746
	14th	725
	21st	715
	28th	732
October	5th	734
	12th	735
	19th	734
	26th	747

SPITFIRE FUNDS

'Spitfire in Memory of Airman Son'

In *The Times* on 19 August, a letter sent to Lord Beaverbrook was reproduced:

On Sunday last we received the tragic news that my son, Flying Officer Norman Merret, had lost his life while serving with the RAF. I cannot provide you with another gallant son. The one who has gone was my only son. But I want you to accept the enclosed cheque to purchase a Spitfire… It is not a personal gift but something to commemorate the passing of my son.

Mr Merret enclosed a cheque for £5,000, which was the publicised 'cost' of a Spitfire. (The real figure was much higher.) Many other individuals and groups donated money to buy Spitfires – some gave their holiday money. These are just ten of the groups who raised funds:

Bolsover Colliery
Cooperative Wholesale Society
Greenock Girls Borstal
Hinckley Hosiery Manufacturers' Association
Women called Dorothy (adverts were placed in *The Times* asking all Dorothys to donate)
People from Cyprus
People from Northern Ireland
People from Stornoway
People from the Gold Coast in West Africa
Police Association of Ontario

£3,050,000

Total raised for purchasing aircraft from public donations by 19 August 1940.

5 MARKS

A Luftwaffe pilot shot down on 1 September was presented with a collection box for the Mayor of Chatham's Spitfire Fund. He gave a 5-Mark note.

RAF MiGs

Britain considered buying fighters from the Soviet Union, but its proposals were not accepted by the Soviets.

Civilian Repair Organisation (CRO)

This organisation was formed in April 1940 and used civilian staff to repair RAF aircraft.

35 per cent

Percentage of total RAF fighter planes sent to squadrons between July and October that had previously been damaged then repaired.

Queen Mary

Nickname for the RAF's long low-loader trailer. It measured 60 feet (18 metres) in length and could carry a complete fighter fuselage.

The Air Forces

RAF

Formed as the world's first independent air force in 1918, the RAF had experienced a huge reduction in machines and personnel during the inter-war years and it was only in 1934 that the government agreed to its expansion. The emphasis was on bombers – the thinking being that aerial bombing had the potential to win wars on its own – and it was not until 1937 that Air Chief Marshal Dowding was able to convince government ministers to strengthen Britain's air defences with fighters.

STRUCTURE

Aircraft within the RAF were organised into four commands:

Fighter Command
Bomber Command

Coastal Command
Training Command

Within Fighter Command, there were groups, then airfield-based sectors with assigned satellite (or forward) airfields under their control, and then, at each airfield, the squadrons. Within each squadron there were two flights, further split into sections.

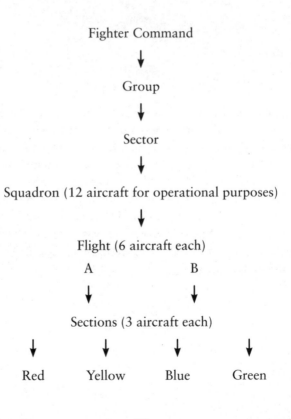

Fighter Command

↓

Group

↓

Sector

↓

Squadron (12 aircraft for operational purposes)

↓

Flight (6 aircraft each)

A   B

↓   ↓

Sections (3 aircraft each)

↓   ↓   ↓   ↓

Red   Yellow   Blue   Green

FIGHTER COMMAND GROUPS

GROUP	AREAS COVERED	COMMANDER
10	South-west England, south Wales	Air Vice-Marshal Quintin Brand
11	South-east England (including London)	Air Vice-Marshal Keith Park
12	Central England, north and central Wales	Air Vice-Marshal Trafford Leigh-Mallory
13	North England, Scotland, Northern Ireland	Air Vice-Marshal Richard Saul

LUFTWAFFE

The Luftwaffe's main role was as an army support force. It had gained experience in the Spanish Civil War as the Condor Legion, during which time one lesson learnt was that accurate bombing was not possible with conventional bombing methods. This was seen to be particularly true at Guernica, in northern Spain, where a bombing raid, which had a road bridge as a primary target, resulted in hundreds of civilian deaths. Now the Luftwaffe was being asked to carry out strategic bombing, a role it hadn't practised for.

STRUCTURE

The Luftwaffe's largest organisational unit was the Luftflotte, composed of aircraft of different types, in contrast to the RAF, which had all its fighters in Fighter Command and all its bombers in Bomber Command.

BATTLE OF BRITAIN LUFTFLOTTE

NAME	LOCATION OF AIRFIELDS	COMMANDER
Luftflotte 2	North-east France, Belgium, Netherlands	Generalfeldmarschall Albert Kesselring
Luftflotte 3	North-west and central France	Generalfeldmarschall Hugo Sperrle
Luftflotte 5	Norway, Denmark	Generalfeldmarschall Hans-Jürgen Stumpff

Luftflotte (air fleet)

↓

2/3 Fliegerkorps (flying corps)

↓

Geschwader: group of 90–120 aircraft,
consisting of 3 Gruppen (wings) and one
Stabschwarm (staff flight)

↓

Gruppe (wing): consisting of 30–40
aircraft based at one airfield, split into
3 or 4 Staffeln (flight squadrons)

↓

Staffel (flight squadron): 10–16 aircraft

GESCHWADER TYPES

ABBREV. /NAME	TRANSLATION	AIRCRAFT
JG/Jagdgeschwader	Hunting group (fighters)	Me 109
ZG/Zerstörergeschwader	Destroyer group	Me 110
KG/Kampfgeschwader	Battle group	He 111, Ju 88, Do 17
StG/Sturzkampfgeschwader	Dive-bomber group	Ju 87

Basic Fighter Formations

FORM-ATION	AIR FORCE	DESCRIPTION	ADVANTAGES/ DISADVANTAGES
Schwarm	Luftwaffe	Four aircraft formed of two pairs (*Rotten*)	Easy to fly, all aircraft were protected and had flexibility to split and rejoin depending on circumstances.
Vic	RAF	Three aircraft in V-shaped formation. Leader with one aircraft flying closely on either side.	Leader couldn't see his wingmen. Others unable to look out for enemy aircraft as busy concentrating on keeping formation.

'Tail-end Charlies'

Name for the pilots who were tasked with weaving behind the RAF fighter squadron's formation. These were often the first to be attacked by Luftwaffe fighters.

'*Idiotenreihen*' ('Rows of Idiots')

German pilots' term for the RAF's 'Vic' formation.

The Defensive System

*I think it is well also for the man in the street to
realise that there is no power on earth that can
protect him from being bombed. Whatever people
may tell him, the bomber will always get through...
The only defence is in offence, which means that you
have to kill more women and children more quickly
than the enemy if you want to save yourselves.*

Stanley Baldwin MP,
House of Commons, 10 November 1932

Britain had been bombed by Gotha bombers and
Zeppelins during the First World War, when over 600
civilians had been killed, and it was feared that future
conflicts would result in deaths on a larger scale, as well
as widespread panic and hysteria. Measures planned to
help protect the civilian population included evacuation,

air-raid shelters and the issuing of gas masks in case of chemical attack.

The Dowding System

Air Chief Marshal Hugh Dowding oversaw the development of the world's first large-scale coordinated air defence system, which relied on a constant feed of information, gained via radar and visual observation, being given to the fighters.

Fighter Command's Operations Room directed the battle by allocating incoming raids to the appropriate Groups. Group HQs then allocated them to the sector stations best placed to respond, who then ordered fighters into the air. Anti-aircraft batteries and barrage balloon units were also alerted.

The system's main advantage was avoiding the need for standing patrols, which required more aircraft than the RAF had available.

Plotting

In the control rooms, raids were monitored on large tables covered with maps of the area by members of the Women's Auxiliary Air Force (WAAF). The movement of raids was plotted using wooden blocks marked with size, heading and altitude, and were moved into position by long croupier sticks. The fighters' positions were also tracked on the same table to allow them to be directed towards the incoming enemy aircraft.

TOTE

The 'tote' was a board in each group and sector operations room that showed the status of each squadron under its control. The states of readiness were illuminated as appropriate for each squadron:

Released (Unavailable)
Available (Could be airborne within 20 minutes)
Ordered to Readiness
At Readiness (Airborne in 5 minutes)
Ordered to Standby
At Standby (Airborne in 2 minutes)
Ordered on 'I' Patrol (A pre-arranged patrol)
Left Ground
In Position
Detailed to Raid
Raid Detail Acknowledged
Ordered to Land
Landed and Refuelling

TERMINOLOGY

Coded words were used in radio communications to and from the fighter pilots. They were introduced to give brevity to the messages and ensure consistency across the different parts of the defensive system.

Angels	altitude ('angels 10' = 10,000 feet)
Bandits	enemy aircraft

Bogey	unidentified aircraft
Scramble	order to take off quickly
Vector	compass direction to take
Buster	instruction to use full throttle
Liner	instruction to use cruising speed
Orbit	instruction to circle over a location
Tally-ho	notification from a pilot who was beginning his attack
Pancake	instruction to return to base

THE BATTLE OF BARKING CREEK

Three days after war was declared, on 6 September 1939, Spitfires were scrambled to intercept detected intruders over Essex, of which two were shot down. Unfortunately they were not German aircraft, but RAF Hurricanes. One pilot, Montague Hulton-Harrop, was killed – the first RAF fatality of the war. The two Spitfire pilots were exonerated at a court martial and the incident was put down to a mistake at a radar filter centre that had confused a returning British aircraft with a German one. The incident led to a review of procedures.

OPERATIONS

It was a race against time for the fighters to reach a sufficient height to gain an advantage over the incoming bombers: attacks were best carried out from above a formation and from the direction of the sun to disguise their approach. RAF fighters were often caught at a disadvantage while climbing to the level of the bombers, being slower at that point than the enemy fighters providing escort to the bombers.

HEAD-ON ATTACKS

111 Squadron used a brave – if dangerous – tactic: they flew in line abreast towards incoming Luftwaffe formations. As German bombers had mainly glass cockpits it had strong psychological effects on their crews. The tactic was later abandoned due to losses sustained.

DEFENSIVE CIRCLE

When attacked, aircraft would form a circle to avoid individual aircraft being picked off. Messerschmitt 110s were particularly noted for doing this.

RADAR

Scientist Robert Watson-Watt, from the small Angus town of Brechin, had been asked to investigate the possibility of producing a death-ray based on radio waves. This idea, based on science fiction rather than science, led to his development of RDF (Radio Direction Finding, later known as radar), which used radio waves to locate flying aircraft.

British radar stations were built near to the coast, but the Luftwaffe was not entirely sure of their purpose.

The Germans listened to RAF fighter radio traffic during interceptions and knew they were being guided from the ground but thought they were only locally controlled and not part of a wider network. They believed the control rooms were underground and so didn't think they'd be able to damage them by aerial bombing. Most control rooms weren't, and were more vulnerable to attack than they realised.

There were two types of fixed radar station:

TYPE	CAPABILITY	DETECTION RANGE	TOWER HEIGHT (TRANSMITTERS)	TYPE
Chain Home	Detecting aircraft at altitude	120 miles	350 feet (107 m)	Fixed
Chain Home Low	To find low-flying aircraft	50 miles	185 feet (56 m)	Rotating aerials

The equipment worked well but it was not without its drawbacks: altitude and formation size were more difficult for the equipment to ascertain than range and bearing. From September the Germans were able to interfere with the signals through electronic jamming, but not to any great effect.

CHAIN HOME STATIONS

CHAIN HOME	CHAIN HOME LOW
Anstruther, Fife	Beachy Head, Sussex
Bamburgh, Northumberland	Caitnip, Orkney
Bawdsey, Suffolk	Carnanton, Cornwall
Bromley, Essex	Cockburnspath,
Canewdon, Essex	Berwickshire
Danby Beacon, Yorkshire	Cresswell, Northumberland
Doonics Hill, Aberdeenshire	Douglas Wood, Angus
Drone Hill, Berwickshire	Dover, Kent
Dunkirk, Kent	Dry Tree, Cornwall
Easington, Yorkshire	Dunwich, Suffolk
Hawk's Tor, Devon	Fairlight, Sussex
Hayscastle Cross,	Flamborough Head,
Pembrokeshire	Yorkshire
High Street, Suffolk	Foreness, Kent
Hillhead, Aberdeenshire	Happisburgh, Norfolk
Nether Button, Orkney	Hopton, Norfolk
Ottercops Moss,	Ingoldmells, Lincolnshire
Northumberland	Poling, Sussex
Pevensey, Sussex	Rame Head, Cornwall
Rye, Sussex	Rosehearty, Aberdeenshire
Schoolhill, Kincardineshire	St Twynnells, Pembrokeshire
Shotton, County Durham	Strumble Head,
St Cyrus, Angus	Pembrokeshire
Staxton Wold, Yorkshire	Truleigh Hill, Sussex
Stenigot, Lincolnshire	Truleigh Hill, Sussex
Stoke Holy Cross, Norfolk	Walton-on-the-Naze, Essex
Thrumster, Caithness	West Prawle, Devon
Ventnor, Isle of Wight	Whitstable, Kent
Warren, Pembrokeshire	
West Beckham, Norfolk	
Worth Matravers, Dorset	

AIR MINISTRY EXPERIMENTAL STATION TYPE I

Official name given to Chain Home stations.

BRITISH SIGHT GRAF ZEPPELIN

*The [German] propaganda ministry said the Graf
Zeppelin was making an experimental flight over
the North Sea last night but expressed surprise that
the airship had been sighted off Scotland… The
flight… had no military purpose, the ministry said.*
St Petersburg Press, Florida, 4 August 1939

The German airship was in fact on an intelligence-gathering
mission, but did not detect the vital radar system.

IFF

An abbreviation of Identification Friend or Foe, this
equipment carried by each RAF aircraft was designed
to differentiate between the appearance of friendly and
enemy aircraft on radar screens.

PIP SQUEAK

The pilots' name for the equipment which controlled the sending from the aircraft's radio of a signal on a specific frequency to be picked up by radar stations, which then triangulated the positions of the fighters.

'IS YOUR COCKEREL CROWING?'

Reminder message from sector controllers to pilots to switch on their Pip Squeak equipment. Cockerel was the official code name.

Y SERVICE

This provided intelligence by listening to Luftwaffe crews' radio messages when they were in the air.

BLETCHLEY PARK

The code breaking at Bletchley Park, Buckinghamshire, played an important contribution in the war, but its role in the battle remains undetermined. One factor that would have prevented operational details being revealed to the Bletchley Park team was that the Luftwaffe used landlines to communicate, which were impervious to radio-based interception.

OBSERVER CORPS

The Observer Corps stemmed from work carried out in the First World War, when policemen sent in reports of enemy aircraft via phone or telegram. In the inter-war years the Observer Corps was established to provide an organised network to visually spot aircraft as they flew inland over Britain. (Radar could not detect targets over land.) Working in teams of two or three, the observers were stationed in open-air observation posts. Using telephones, they passed on the following information:

Direction
Height
Number of aircraft
Type of aircraft (Friendly/Hostile/Unrecognised)

If aircraft could not be seen but were nonetheless heard, a report of their sounds was given.

30,000

Members of the Observer Corps. Most were volunteers who combined their duties with full-time jobs. Around 4,000 were women.

1,000

Number of observation posts around the country.

OBSERVATION POST EQUIPMENT

Telephone
Observer instrument
Table
Tripod legs
Tripod head
Tripod shoes
Canvas instrument cover
Canvas tripod cover
Sunglasses
Binoculars (with case and strap)
Torch

At one post a bomb dropped within 50 yards but the Observers on duty were so busy plotting that they did not notice it. At another, where a bomb dropped closer, I have been informed that I am to be asked to supply a new pair of trousers.

Circular sent by Air Commodore Warrington-Morris,
Observer Corps Commandant, June 1940

ANTI-AIRCRAFT DEFENCES

ARTILLERY

Anti-aircraft artillery batteries had an important role to play in hitting incoming bombers or at least disrupting their bombing runs. They were deployed around important targets but were short in numbers. Accuracy was not helped by the lack of radar-assisted targeting, but aircraft were brought down and, perhaps more importantly, civilian morale was boosted by the guns going off during raids.

GUNS

TYPE	NUMBER RECOMMENDED	NUMBER IN SERVICE (BY END OF JULY)
Heavy anti-aircraft	2,232	1,280
Light anti-aircraft	1,860	517

The deficiency in numbers didn't improve: in the second half of 1940 only an average of 40 heavy guns were supplied each month.

1,466

Number of barrage balloons in use by the end of July 1940. A third were stationed around London.

4,000

Number of searchlights in operation across the country. They could be effective in blinding enemy aircrews but were ineffective at altitudes above 12,000 feet.

Parachute and Cable Device (PAC)

As low-flying enemy aircraft approached, lengths of 480-feet-long (146-metre-long) metal cable, with explosive devices attached, were fired into the air by rocket and then suspended under a parachute. It was used successfully at RAF Kenley, where several enemy aircraft set off the explosive devices attached to the cables.

Pre-battle

PHONEY WAR

Engagements between British and German forces were infrequent following the beginning of the war in September 1939 and led to the period up to the spring of 1940 being termed the 'Phoney War'. Both sides held back their aerial forces, with only reconnaissance flights taking place in addition to some small raids launched by the Germans.

NORWAY

In April 1940 Germany invaded Denmark and Norway, the latter seeing a fragmented and disjointed response by the British, which resulted in heavy losses amongst those sent across the North Sea. A squadron of outdated Gloster Gladiator biplanes and all of 46 Squadron's Hurricanes were lost when the aircraft carrier HMS *Glorious* was sunk by German battleships.

BATTLE OF FRANCE

The long-awaited assault began on 10 May as Hitler launched his invasion of France and the Low Countries. The British army, in the form of the British Expeditionary Force, was supported by RAF aircraft as it faced the invading forces alongside the French army and air force.

FALL GELB (CASE YELLOW)

German name for the invasion.

BLITZKRIEG (LIGHTNING WAR)

This German strategy utilised tanks as the spearhead, being supported by artillery, aircraft and infantry. The Allies had almost parity in numbers of armoured vehicles and troops, but were at a disadvantage in terms of aircraft, and cooperation between the two Allied armies was not always effective in the face of the German onslaught. The Germans were well organised and more tactically astute and pulled off a masterstroke in surprising the Allies by advancing through the Ardennes forest. They crossed the Meuse river and moved north towards the English Channel, which they reached just 10 days after the start of the overall offensive.

56 PER CENT

Loss rate of RAF Battle and Blenheim bombers sent to attack bridges at Sedan in northern France on 14 May. The bombers were slow and weakly armed and, when unescorted, especially vulnerable to German fighters.

83

Number of Luftwaffe aircraft shot down by French and RAF aircraft on 10 May – the highest loss rate of any day in 1940.

ROGER BUSHELL

One of the pilots shot down and taken prisoner on 23 May. In March 1944 he led 'the Great Escape' from Stalag Luft III, after which he was recaptured and, along with 49 others, shot on Hitler's orders.

5

Typical number of sorties being flown each day by Hurricane pilots. While there were many available targets, the RAF pilots were outnumbered by those of the Luftwaffe. Spitfires were held back in Britain, their narrow-track undercarriage deemed too risky for the rougher French airfields. Throughout the Battle of France there was pressure from the French for more

British fighters to be sent, but this was resisted by British commanders, especially Dowding.

DOWDING MEMORANDUM

Dowding was determined to hold onto as many aircraft as possible for home defence, rather than see them needlessly destroyed in France. He wrote a famous memorandum to Harold Balfour, Under Secretary of State for Air, on 16 May:

I must therefore request that as a matter of paramount urgency the Air Ministry will consider and decide what level of strength is to be left to the Fighter Command for the defences of this country, and will assure me that when this level has been reached, not one fighter will be sent across the Channel however urgent and insistent the appeals for help may be.

I believe that, if an adequate fighter force is kept in this country, if the fleet remains in being, and if Home Forces are suitably organised to resist invasion, we should be able to carry on the war single handed for some time, if not indefinitely. But, if the Home Defence Force is drained away in desperate attempts to remedy the situation in France, defeat in France will involve the final, complete and irremediable defeat of this country.

DUNKIRK

The German advance had cut off the French and British forces, who withdrew and were encircled at the port of Dunkirk. The situation hopeless, an evacuation was planned. On 24 May the panzers were halted, as Göring had promised his bombers that they could finish off the Allied armies. However, bad weather and the efforts of the RAF prevented this from taking place and Royal Navy and civilian ships were able to carry out a massive evacuation effort, which ended on 4 June.

338,226

Number of Allied troops evacuated from the beaches and harbour at Dunkirk.

'WHERE WAS THE RAF?'

Sailors and soldiers criticised the RAF for not being seen over the beaches, but they did not have enough aircraft or pilots to carry out constant patrols. Fighters also operated away from the embarkation area. A crucial disadvantage was that Britain's radar-based fighter-control system was not effective over northern France and so the RAF were operating blind.

If we hadn't been there I don't think many of them would have got out.
Flight Sergeant George Unwin, 19 Squadron

155

Number of Spitfires lost covering the evacuation.

ON THE BEACHES

With the Dunkirk evacuation complete, Winston Churchill gave his famous speech in Parliament on 4 June that included a resolute statement of intent:

We shall go on to the end, we shall fight in France, we shall fight on the seas and oceans, we shall fight with growing confidence and growing strength in the air, we shall defend our Island, whatever the cost may be, we shall fight on the beaches, we shall fight on the landing grounds, we shall fight in the fields and in the streets, we shall fight in the hills; we shall never surrender.

LOSSES (10 MAY TO 20 JUNE)

Both sides suffered large losses and time was needed to regroup and replenish.

	AIRCRAFT	AIRCREW
Luftwaffe	1,428	3,059
RAF (All Commands)	944	915

66

Number of Hurricanes that returned to Britain out of the 261 sent to France to support the British Expeditionary Force. Over a hundred had to be destroyed by ground crews in the forced retreat.

362

Number of pilots Fighter Command was short of its full establishment on 15 June.

Thank God we're alone now.

Air Chief Marshal Hugh Dowding, following the French surrender on 22 June

Invasion

We are very close to the end of the war.
Josef Goebbels, 23 June 1940

QUICK STRIKE

*We couldn't understand why the enemy
didn't come for us at once.*
Wing Commander Ronald Adams

With France defeated, some German commanders argued for a quick attack on Britain while its depleted forces were recovering. They wanted to use airborne forces to capture airfields but the Luftwaffe had also suffered heavy losses and needed time to move into its new bases in occupied France.

I do not intend to carry out Sea Lion.
There is no bridge across the sea. On land
I'm a hero, on sea I'm a coward.
Hitler to Field Marshal von Runstedt, July 1940

In the weeks following the defeat of France, Hitler showed no signs of urgency. There was no overarching war plan that guided German action; it was left to Hitler to decide and he hoped peace with Britain would come without military action. This led to inactivity, as his commanders did not know what to do next.

INVASION PLANS

The German Navy had looked at the potential of a seaborne invasion in September 1939, but it had not been seriously considered until first discussed in May 1940, when German Navy chief Grand Admiral Erich Raeder raised the subject with Hitler. Raeder preferred the less risky option of setting up a blockade using U-boats, navy ships and Luftwaffe aircraft. Invasion was regarded as a last resort: it was hoped that bombing – which had been effective for the Germans at Warsaw in 1939 and Rotterdam in 1940 – could force Britain to sue for peace. Göring believed his Luftwaffe alone would defeat Britain's resolve.

1,297

Number of French sailors killed at Mers-el-Kébir in French Algeria on 3 July when Royal Navy warships attacked the French fleet. Churchill had ordered the operation to prevent the ships falling into German hands. This ruthless action against an ally sent a message of Britain's resolve to continue the war.

FÜHRER DIRECTIVE NUMBER 16

Discussions had taken place between German commanders and on 16 July Hitler issued a directive, which included these sections:

As Britain, despite her hopeless military situation,
still shows no sign of willingness to come to terms,
I have decided to prepare a landing operation
against Britain and, if necessary, to carry it out.
The aim of this operation is to eliminate the
British motherland as a base from which
war against Germany can be continued and,
if necessary, to occupy it completely.

The British air force must be so far neutralised, both
actually and in morale, that it will offer no appreciable
resistance to the German crossing operation.
Preparations for the operation must
be completed by mid August.

UNTERNEHMEN SEELÖWE (OPERATION SEA LION)

German name assigned to the invasion.

'SMITH'

Code name assigned to the invasion by the British until 'Sea Lion' was known.

REQUIREMENTS

The landings were to be carried out with certain criteria in place:

> 2 hours before high water
> A sea state less than 2
> At dawn
> With light from a half-moon

This meant that possible dates were limited. The invasion also had to take place before the poorer weather of late autumn.

MINES

Sea lanes would have to be cleared of British mines and the approach routes would have to be protected by German mines. The German Navy was, however, unable to guarantee the crossing would be free of the British mine threat.

ANTON, BRUNO, CAESAR AND DORA

Names of German minefields that would be established to protect the invasion fleet.

698

Number of British minesweepers in September 1940. The Royal Navy was a potent naval power and was well equipped to deal with German mines.

AIR SUPREMACY

It was essential to the German commanders that the Royal Air Force – as well as British naval forces and harbours – was put out of action before any invasion could begin. The plan relied on the Luftwaffe's ability to defeat its British counterpart.

TROOPS AND RESOURCES
(FIRST ARMY PLAN, ISSUED 25 JULY)

The first wave would consist of 13 divisions, to be landed in two echelons. Three further waves would bring another 17 infantry, six armoured and three motorised divisions.

	FIRST ECHELON	SECOND ECHELON
Men	90,000	170,000

Tanks	650	-
Horses	4,500	57,500
Vehicles	-	34,200
Field guns	-	500

10 Days

Time the German Navy stated it would take to land all the troops of the first wave. This was unacceptable to the German Army commanders, who knew this would leave the landed troops exposed and at a disadvantage.

Broad Front or Narrow Front?

The landing must be effected in the form of a mighty river-crossing on a broad front.
General Alfred Jodl, Chief of German High
Command Operations Staff, 12 July

There were divisions amongst the German High Command: the navy wanted as narrow a front as possible in order to allow better protection for the ships in the Channel; the army wanted as wide a front as possible for tactical reasons.

I utterly reject the Navy's proposal; from the point of view of the Army I regard their proposal as complete suicide. I might just as well put the troops that have been landed straight through the sausage machine.
Colonel-General Franz Halder,
Chief of Army General Staff, 7 August

FRONT WIDTH

225 MILES	50 MILES	80 MILES
Army's initial planned width	Navy's suggestion	Agreed compromise width

LANDING SITES

On 27 August Hitler decided on the final invasion plan. The 13 divisions on the initial plan were reduced to nine and would be landed in four zones:

FIRST WAVE	LANDING ZONES			
	E	D	C	B
Area (west to east)	Selsey Bill to Worthing	Beachy Head to Bexhill	Hastings to Rye	Dungeness to Folkestone
Width of landing area (miles)	21	11	11	14
Embarkation ports	Le Havre	Boulogne	Calais	Rotterdam, Dunkirk, Ostend
Army forces (divisions)*	3	2	2	2

*One additional airborne division was to be dropped near to Folkestone.

If the invasion worked, then a further 400,000 men would be sent over to join the advance.

UNTERNEHMEN HERBSTREISE (OPERATION AUTUMN JOURNEY)

This diversion would see German ships sailing towards the coast between Aberdeen and north-east England before turning round, and before they could be intercepted and the ruse blown too soon. It was hoped a sizeable part of the Royal Navy Home Fleet would be tied down through this ploy.

INVASION SHIPPING

German vessels required to transport men and equipment across the Channel:

	PLANNED NUMBER	NUMBER REQUISITIONED BY 4 SEPTEMBER
Barges	1,722	1,910
Tugs	471	419
Motorboats	1,161	1,600
Transport ships	155	168

BARGES

Along with the other vessels, barges were commandeered from all over occupied German territory. They were converted to allow a front-loading ramp; Germany didn't have any specialised landing craft. The barges were low in the water and vulnerable to heavy seas. Crossing the Channel in a flat-bottomed vessel would not have been a pleasant experience for the men on board.

4 KNOTS

Maximum speed of the transport barges.

12 MILES

Projected length of the Boulogne invasion force as it crossed the Channel.

THE BLACKPOOL FRONT

Term used by RAF bomber crews for continental Channel ports, due to the fires they had started and the ensuing glow being visible from a great distance.

36 PER CENT

Percentage of all sorties flown by RAF Bomber Command between July and October against continental Channel ports and the invasion shipping being prepared there.

12 PER CENT

Percentage of invasion barges destroyed by RAF bombers.

NAVY FORCES

The surface forces are so weak and so few in number against the British fleet that the only course open to them is to show that they know how to die gallantly.
Grand Admiral Erich Raeder, 3 September 1939

The German Navy was wary of the whole seaborne operation and thought the entire invasion army force could be lost. They were well aware of the overwhelming strength of the Royal Navy and their inability to do much to counter it: during the invasion build-up, British ships were able to shell German-held ports with near impunity.

The German Navy had calculated it would take too long to ferry all the troops across the Channel and were worried the Luftwaffe would not be able to defend the invasion force. Their main concern was they didn't have enough ships after suffering heavy losses during the invasion of Norway in April.

DESTROYERS AVAILABLE

German Navy	10
Royal Navy (Home Fleet)	80

As preparations continued, the hopes of Germany's military commanders rested on the Luftwaffe to produce the decisive result.

Air War against Britain

*What General Weygand has called the Battle of France
is over; the Battle of Britain is about to begin...
Let us therefore brace ourselves to our duty, and
so bear ourselves that if the British Empire and
its Commonwealth last for a thousand years,
men will still say, 'This was their finest hour.'*
Winston Churchill, 18 June

LUFTWAFFE STRATEGY

Reichsmarschall Göring issued an operational directive
entitled the 'General Directive for the Operation of the
Luftwaffe against Britain' on 30 June. It outlined the
immediate aims of the Luftwaffe:

Attack aircraft industry targets
Attack RAF airfields and its facilities
Evaluate the strength of British defences
Attack harbours and facilities
Attack merchant shipping and Royal Navy warships
    to cut imports.

The Luftwaffe was expected to achieve much and, although it had not fully recovered its losses from the earlier campaigns, it still was a numerically superior force. It also suffered a major drawback, however: its bombers had not been conceived to be a strategic bombing force and therefore lacked the capability to carry heavy bomb loads.

Throughout the campaign bomber crews were ordered to avoid causing unnecessary civilian casualties, and some 'nuisance' night-time bombing, which gave crews practice of attacking Britain, had already taken place in June and July on targets across the country.

Luftwaffe figures such as fighter pilot Adolf Galland and Field Marshal Erhard Milch believed Britain could only be defeated if its fighters were first eliminated from the battle. They felt Luftwaffe operations were to lure Fighter Command to the skies, where they thought it could be beaten.

Aircraft at Front-line Squadrons
(Beginning of July)

TYPE	RAF	LUFTWAFFE
Single-seat fighters:	754	1,107
Two-seat fighters:	149	357
Bombers	560	1,808
Reconnaissance	-	569
TOTAL:	1,468	3,841

The British single-seat fighters – the Spitfires and Hurricanes – were outnumbered by their opponents 5 to 1.

RAF Fighter Command Squadrons
(Beginning of July)

AIRCRAFT	SQUADRONS
Hurricane	29
Spitfire	19
Blenheim	8
Defiant	2
TOTAL	58

First Phase
(10 July–11 August)

The first phase of the battle saw the Luftwaffe attack British shipping in the English Channel, as well as other targets including ports, factories, railways and airfields. They aimed to test defences and find out how strong the RAF was. They hoped the RAF would suffer losses as a result of challenging these small-scale attacks and that they would gain air superiority over the Channel area.

These raids were a learning experience for the RAF and allowed it to improve its defensive systems before the main aerial offensive began. As a result of the Germans sending formations to different areas at the same time, commander of 11 Group, Air Vice-Marshal Keith Park, learnt to deploy his fighters in small groups, so as to avoid all his resources being sent to raids that were actually feints.

KANALKAMPF (CHANNEL BATTLE)

What the Germans called the battle for air superiority in the Channel area.

FIGHTER COMMAND ORDER OF BATTLE, 10 JULY 1940

GROUP	SECTOR STATIONS (AIRCRAFT TYPE & SQUADRON)	SATELLITE/FORWARD AIRFIELDS (AIRCRAFT TYPE & SQUADRON)
10	Filton	**Exeter** Hurricane: 87, 213 **Pembrey** Spitfire: 92 **St Eval** Spitfire: 234
	Middle Wallop Spitfire: 609 Hurricane: 238	

11	**Biggin Hill** Hurricane: 32 Defiant: 141	**Gravesend** Spitfire: 610 Blenheim: 604 **Manston** Blenheim: 600
	Debden Hurricane: 17	
	Hornchurch Spitfire: 65, 74	**Rochford** Spitfire: 54
	Kenley Spitfire: 64 Hurricane: 615	**Croydon** Hurricane: 111, 501
	Northolt Hurricane: 1 Blenheim: 604	**Hendon** Hurricane: 257
	North Weald Hurricane: 56, 151	**Martlesham Heath** Hurricane: 85 Blenheim: 25
	Tangmere Hurricane: 43, 145, 601	

12	**Coltishall** Spitfire: 66 Hurricane: 242	
	Digby Spitfire: 611 Hurricane: 46 Blenheim: 29	
	Duxford Defiant: 264	**Fowlmere** Spitfire: 19
	Kirton-in-Lindsey Spitfire: 222	
	Wittering Hurricane: 229 Spitfire: 266	**Collyweston** Blenheim: 23
13	**Catterick** Spitfire: 41 Blenheim: 219	
	Church Fenton Hurricane: 73 Spitfire: 616	**Leconfield** Hurricane: 249
	Dyce Hurricane: 263	
	Turnhouse Spitfire: 603 Hurricane: 79, 245, 253,	**Drem** Spitfire: 602 Hurricane: 605
	Usworth Hurricane: 607	**Acklington** Spitfire: 72, 152
	Wick Hurricane: 3	**Castletown** Hurricane: 504

NOTABLE DAYS OF THE BATTLE: 10 JULY

Raids had started on shipping in June and on 4 July the first major air attack had taken place on Portland naval base, but it wasn't until 10 July that a concentrated effort from the Luftwaffe began.

'BREAD'

Code name for convoy that passed through the Dover Straits. Five fighter squadrons were vectored to meet the incoming bombers. The ensuing aerial engagements heralded the start of the Battle of Britain.

FIRST BATTLE CASUALTY

During a dogfight over the Channel, Flying Officer Tom Higgs of 111 Squadron hit an enemy Dornier 17, either through ramming or by accident, and the collision caused his left wing to break off. He baled out, but his body was found on the Dutch coast four weeks later. He was the first RAF combat casualty of the battle.

30

Number of civilians killed in a bombing raid on Swansea.

FLARE ATTACK

When First World War veteran pilot Wing Commander Ira Jones heard of the Swansea raid he pursued the bombers in an unarmed Hawker Henley target tug aircraft, armed with only a flare pistol, but did not reach firing range. (A target tug tows a target so that fighter pilots can get aerial target practice.)

Losses

	AIRCRAFT	AIRCREW (KILLED)
Luftwaffe	11	29
Fighter Command	2	2

Oh! Here's one coming down. There's one going down in flames. Somebody's hit a German and he's coming down with a long streak, coming down completely out of control... a long streak of smoke. And now a man's baled out by parachute.
BBC reporter Charles Gardner, 14 July

Gardner gave a live radio commentary on a convoy attack off Dover. The pilot he saw baling out was in fact a British pilot who died the next day. The BBC journalist was criticised by some for his overenthusiastic reporting.

HELL'S CORNER

Name given to an area near Dover and Folkestone due to the heavy fighting there.

A LAST APPEAL TO REASON

Hitler made a speech on 19 July at the Reichstag where he outlined Germany's successes so far and appealed to Britain to end the war. His speech was reproduced in leaflets dropped on Britain by the Luftwaffe:

> *I feel it to be my duty before my own conscience
> to appeal once more to reason and common
> sense in Great Britain as much as elsewhere. I
> consider myself in a position to make this appeal,
> since I am not the vanquished, begging favours,
> but the victor speaking in the name of reason. I
> can see no reason why this war must go on. I am
> grieved to think of the sacrifices it will claim.*

BBC broadcaster Sefton Delmer offered an immediate and unofficial response (which turned out to reflect the official views which were communicated later):

> *Herr Führer, we hurl it right back at you,
> right in your evil-smelling teeth.*

SLAUGHTER OF THE INNOCENTS

Name given to events on 19 July when nine Defiants of
141 Squadron were sent to intercept a convoy raid on
their first sortie. Six were shot down; killing 10 aircrew.
On this day Fighter Command lost a total of ten aircraft
to the Luftwaffe's four – a rare day when the RAF's
losses were higher than those of their counterparts.

NAMES GIVEN TO 141 SQUADRON'S DEFIANTS

Cock o' the North
Cock-a-Hoop
Cocksure
Cocked for Firing

BOSOM TO BOSHAM

As convoy 'Bosom' was moving through the Channel
on 20 July, one of its escorting squadrons was missing.
601 Squadron commander Sir Archibald Hope had
misheard and led his fighters to orbit over Bosham. By
the time the mistake was realised his fighters had missed
their rendezvous.

2

Number of ships that arrived undamaged on 25 July at
Portland from the 21 that had set off as convoy CW.8.
At one point Stukas were able to attack unhindered

as they arrived just as British fighters were retiring to refuel following a dogfight.

504

Number of sorties flown by 54 Squadron in the three weeks up until 26 July. The squadron had only five surviving members of the 17 pilots they had had at the start of the Dunkirk evacuation.

HMS *Wren* & HMS *Codrington*

Two Royal Navy destroyers sunk by the Luftwaffe on 27 July. *Codrington* was in port at Dover and German attacks on the naval base led to the navy withdrawing from using it. It was a sign the Germans were winning the Channel battle.

Führer Directive Number 17

The Luftwaffe is to overpower the British
Air Force with all the forces at its command,
in the shortest possible time.
Adolf Hitler, 1 August

Earlier orders had targeted coastal ports and British ships, and now the RAF was to be attacked: its airfields and aircraft, followed by armament factories and then harbours (leaving those needed for the invasion).

Shipping attacks were to be reduced. The Luftwaffe was to be ready to support the invasion. Hitler's order stated that 'the intensification of the air war may commence on or after 5 August. The exact time is to be decided by the Luftwaffe after the completion of preparations and in the light of the weather.'

4 Days

On 6 August, Göring and his commanders agreed a strategy to destroy Fighter Command in southern Britain in four days. The Luftwaffe interpreted Directive Number 17 as meaning Fighter Command was the chief priority and targets that might aid the landings could be given lower priority. Once the aerial defences had been eliminated, factories and other military targets would be attacked. The offensive was to be called *Adlerangriff* (Eagle Attack) and would begin on *Adlertag* (Eagle Day).

NOTABLE DAYS OF THE BATTLE: 8 AUGUST

To all units of Luftflotten 2, 3 and 5. Within a short period you will wipe the British Air Force from the sky.
Reichsmarschall Hermann Göring, Order of the Day, 8 August

The last major engagement in the Channel battle took place on 8 August. A lull in aerial activity had encouraged the sending of a coal-carrying convoy CW.9 (code-named *Peewit*), which was sailing westwards towards Dorset. Three boats were sunk by German

E-boats in the morning and then the Luftwaffe sent in its bombers. The biggest aerial fighting of the battle so far took place.

Freya

Code name for German mobile radar units used to look across the Channel for ship convoys. *Peewit*'s location was detected by Freya, which the British didn't realise was being used.

262

Number of German bombers and escorts that took part in the attacks.

4

Number of *Peewit* ships that remained undamaged from the 20 that set out.

Losses

	AIRCRAFT	AIRCREW (KILLED)
Luftwaffe	24	30
Fighter Command	21	20

TARGET PORTLAND

Following the heavy fighting of 8 August there was a lull, lasting a few days. On the morning of 11 August, the largest formation seen so far attacked Portland naval base.

165

Number of Luftwaffe aircraft in the Portland raid. They were met by 74 RAF fighters.

25

Number of Fighter Command aircrew killed on 11 August – its highest daily toll of the battle.

First Phase Losses (10 July–11 August)

Fighter Command had been forced to fly standing patrols, which involved long periods of flying over the convoys. They were heavy on resources and costly. Pilots felt their efforts were wasted on convoys carrying materials that could be carried by train.

	AIRCRAFT	AIRCREW (KILLED)
Luftwaffe	309	519
Fighter Command	163	123

30,000

Shipping tonnage sank by the Luftwaffe during the Channel battle.

Second Phase (12–23 August)

In this phase the Luftwaffe changed their focus and attacked forward RAF airfields and radar stations. Large formations would attack dispersed targets at the same time, a strategy designed to stretch Fighter Command's resources to breaking point.

FIGHTER FORCES (10 AUGUST)

	SINGLE-ENGINED FIGHTERS AVAILABLE FOR COMBAT
Fighter Command	749
Luftwaffe	805

These RAF aircraft were stationed around Britain, while the Luftwaffe's were concentrated just across the Channel.

RADAR ATTACKS

On 12 August a low-level raid saw Messerschmitt 110s fly down the Channel then suddenly turn in towards their radar-station targets on the south coast:

Dover	put out of action
Rye	put out of action
Pevensey	put out of action
Dunkirk	undamaged

A gap was thereby created in the defence system, which allowed following formations through that same day. The airfields at Lympne and Hawkinge were also hit, then the city of Portsmouth. While the three radar stations that had been hit were being put back into operation in the hours that followed, another, Ventnor (on the Isle of Wight) was attacked. Later in the day the RAF station at Manston in Kent was bombed for the first time.

11 Days

Length of time the radar station at Ventnor was out of action. Dummy signals were sent to give the impression it was still operational.

ERPROBUNGSGRUPPE 210

A specialist Luftwaffe unit that carried out accurate, small-scale raids, including those on the radar sites on 12 August.

ESCORT DUTIES

At one point in the raid the German fighters flying as high escort held off their attack, as they didn't think the RAF were yet making their main response. As they delayed, ten of their bombers were shot down.

NOTABLE DAYS OF THE BATTLE: 13 AUGUST, *ADLERTAG* (EAGLE DAY)

Having been postponed due to bad weather, the launch of the major Luftwaffe offensive now saw large-scale attacks on RAF airfields. Their aim was to destroy Fighter Command, although some Luftwaffe commanders were confused about whether they were to bomb them on the ground or destroy them in the air. This lack of a clear strategy led to a misdirection of effort: airfields were attacked which weren't part of Fighter Command.

Raids in the morning were postponed due to poor weather, but not all participating aircraft were told in time as escorting Luftwaffe fighters were unable to communicate with the airborne bombers. They had no shared radio capability. In the afternoon large raids were mounted but it was not the glorious success that Göring had hoped for.

Stations attacked:
Eastchurch (Coastal Command)
Odiham (Fighter Command)
Andover (Maintenance Command)
Farnborough (Royal Aircraft Establishment)
Detling (Coastal Command).

'ACHTUNG! ACHTUNG! SPIT UND HURRI!'

Luftwaffe bomber commander overheard on radio by RAF pilots.

UNLUCKY 13

On this day, 609 Squadron's 13 pilots shot down 13 Luftwaffe aircraft.

1,485

Number of sorties flown by the Luftwaffe – the largest daily total so far.

70 PER CENT

Loss rate of one Stuka squadron.

67

Number of personnel killed when a mess block was hit at RAF Detling.

700 PER CENT

Luftwaffe overestimation of RAF losses on 13 August. Both sides overclaimed the aircraft they had shot down.

The difficulties in determining exact numbers were exacerbated by many of the aircraft ending up in the Channel. One result of the exaggerated numbers claimed was the Germans having heightened expectations of the RAF's collapse.

If the Germans' figures were accurate they would be in London in a week, otherwise they would not.
Air Chief Marshal Hugh Dowding to Archibald
Sinclair, Secretary of State for Air

Losses

	AIRCRAFT	AIRCREW (KILLED)
Luftwaffe	39	66
Fighter Command	15	4

On 14 August poor weather prevented any large-scale raids taking place in the morning. In the afternoon small groups of German bombers attacked various targets: the Varne Lightship in the Dover Straits was bombed and sunk.

NOTABLE DAYS OF THE BATTLE: 15 AUGUST

Luftwaffe commanders assumed the RAF was weakened and planned to stretch it to potential breaking point.

Raids were launched throughout the day on a wide front, from airports in France and all the way up to Norway, by all three Luftflotten. A day of hectic action saw airfields, radar stations and other targets hit.

Hawkinge and Lympne

These two Fighter Command forward stations were put out of action for several days by Stukas.

Radar Gap

The radar stations at Rye, Dover and Foreness were all put out of operation when bombs cut the power cables. A Messerschmitt 110 formation made its way through the ensuing gap in defensive coverage and was able to bomb RAF Manston. RAF Martlesham Heath was also successfully attacked by low-level Messerschmitt 109s acting as fighter-bombers; the airfield was closed for two days. Once the 109s had dropped their bombs they reverted to their normal fighter role and shot down three RAF fighters on the way home.

Despite their initial success the Germans made a major mistake in not following up radar site attacks. Another mistake the Luftwaffe command made was in not ordering follow-up raids on airfields. They assumed their attacks had put them out of action. This allowed the bases to be repaired.

It is doubtful whether there is any point in continuing the attacks on radar sites, in view of the fact that not one of those attacked has been put out of action.
Reichsmarschall Hermann Göring, 15 August

LUFTFLOTTE 5

Flying from Norway towards targets in the north of England, Luftflotte 5's bombers had to fly without Messerschmitt 109 escorts as the fighters did not have sufficient range. Messerschmitt 110s acted as protectors instead, but they were not successful. From one unit alone (I/ZG76), seven were shot down.

20 PER CENT

Aircraft loss rate of Luftflotte 5. It did not make any further daylight raids.

1,786

Number of sorties flown by the Luftwaffe – the highest by either side during the battle.

'BLACK THURSDAY'

Luftwaffe name for 15 August. Their worst day of losses was not offset by operational success.

GERMAN AIRMAN'S PLEA

A German airman of about 18 years who baled out from his machine in the south-east of England produced a photograph from his breast pocket when he was caught. He held it up and said 'This is my mother'. He explained that he had been told that if he showed a photograph of his mother the English would not shoot him.

The Times, 15 August

Losses

	AIRCRAFT	AIRCREW (KILLED)
Luftwaffe	76	128
Fighter Command	35	11

NOTABLE DAYS OF THE BATTLE: 16 AUGUST

Another day of heavy raids. The Germans showed tactical ingenuity when a large formation in the afternoon broke into four smaller ones, one of which hit RAF Tangmere, causing widespread damage.

1,715

Number of sorties flown by the Luftwaffe.

4 Days

Length of time RAF West Malling was put out of action after heavy bombing.

66

Number killed in a raid on London's docks. For the second day in a row the capital had been bombed, following a raid on Croydon airfield the previous day.

Ruse

At RAF Brize Norton two Junkers Ju 88 bombers approached with their wheels down, hoping to be misidentified as British bombers. The ruse worked and they were able to destroy 46 aircraft on the ground.

PORTSMOUTH, GOSPORT AND LEE-ON-SOLENT

These three naval targets were bombed, causing casualties and damage, particularly at Portsmouth.

JAMES NICOLSON, VC

During an engagement with the enemy near Southampton on 16th August 1940, Flight Lieutenant Nicolson's aircraft was hit by four cannon shells, two of which wounded him whilst another set fire to the gravity tank. When about to abandon his aircraft owing to flames in the cockpit he sighted an enemy fighter. This he attacked and shot down, although as a result of staying in his burning aircraft he sustained serious burns to his hands, face, neck and legs.

Medal citation, *London Gazette*, 15 November

As Nicolson descended by parachute he was further wounded by a Home Guard sergeant firing a shotgun. The sergeant was subsequently beaten up by others arriving at the scene. Nicolson recovered from his injuries but was killed in an air accident in May 1945. He was the only Fighter Command recipient of the Victoria Cross during the war.

THE FEW

Churchill visited Fighter Command's operations room at Uxbridge on 16 August and saw that they had no reserves available – all squadrons were in action. As he was driven away, he uttered a line to his chief of staff that he would repeat a few days later in the House of Commons: 'Never in the field of human conflict was so much owed by so many to so few.' RAF fighter pilots joked that it referred to their bar bills.

300

On 16 August, Luftwaffe intelligence claimed that Fighter Command only had 300 aircraft left – it had over twice that in operational readiness.

Losses

	AIRCRAFT	AIRCREW (KILLED)
Luftwaffe	44	55
Fighter Command	24	11

I am having the time of my life. I would not swap places with a king. Peacetime is going to be very boring after this!
Leutnant Hans-Otto Lessing, JG51, writing on 17 August. He was shot down and killed the next day.

Notable Days of the Battle: 18 August

Another day of heavy raids, with almost a thousand Luftwaffe sorties.

P3059, P3815, N2617, P3208

Serial numbers of four 501 Squadron Hurricanes shot down in as many minutes by Oberleutnant Gerhard Schöpfel.

'Having a Sore Neck'

Phrase used to describe ambitious Luftwaffe fighter pilots who were keen to win the Knight's Cross of the Iron Cross, as the medal was worn around the neck.

First Targets

RAF stations Biggin Hill and Kenley were the first to be attacked.

80 TONS

Weight of bombs dropped on Biggin Hill. Most missed their targets, landing on a nearby golf course. Some were found by bomb disposal experts to be British bombs, left behind in France earlier in the summer.

9 TONS

Weight of bombs dropped on RAF Kenley. All hangars were destroyed.

2 HOURS

Length of time Kenley was out of action.

9

Number of RAF personnel killed at Kenley.

4

Number of Hurricanes destroyed on the ground at Kenley.

'GET ME HOME'

Cry from Dornier pilot hit in the chest in the attack on Kenley.

ATTACKS IN THE SOUTH-WEST

The battle then shifted as the Luftwaffe attacked in the south-west. Luftwaffe intelligence had misidentified the targeted airfields: none were in Fighter Command and any damage they caused would not affect the main battle.

Gosport	Fleet Air Arm
Ford	Fleet Air Arm
Thorney Island	Coastal Command

28

Number killed at Ford. No warning had been given of the attack.

18

Number of Stukas lost out of the 109 that attacked Gosport, Ford and Thorney Island. The heavy losses led to the type being withdrawn from front-line action.

'DROP IN FOR A BATH ANY TIME, M'BOY'

Lord Cornwallis to RAF pilot Robert Stanford Tuck after he had been looked after at His Lordship's country house, having been shot down nearby.

TURNED BACK

The early evening saw more raids and heavy fighting as the bombers headed for RAF Hornchurch and other targets in the Thames area. Forbidden to bomb London, they turned back when cloud obscured the targets.

Losses

	AIRCRAFT	AIRCREW (KILLED)
Luftwaffe	67	97
Fighter Command	33*	10

*29 non-Fighter Command aircraft were also lost.

'THE HARDEST DAY'

Name given by historian Alfred Price to 18 August, as the combined losses were the largest of all days in the battle.

REVIEW OF PROGRESS

We have reached the decisive period of the air war against Britain. The vital task is to turn all means at our disposal to the defeat of the enemy air force.
Reichsmarschall Hermann Göring, 19 August

Both the Luftwaffe and the RAF reviewed their progress on 19 August. Göring was perturbed by the losses and Stukas were withdrawn from action unless conditions were favourable. Bombers were to be escorted more closely. This meant fighters would use up more fuel, forcing them to turn back early, leaving bombers unescorted for part of their missions. Luftflotte 3's Me 109s were moved to escort Luftflotte 2's bombers; Luftflotte 3 was to concentrate on night raids. Göring also shook up the command structure: notable fighter pilots such as Adolf Galland were promoted to Jagdgeschwader commanders.

The Luftwaffe's priority targets were to be:

RAF Fighter Command
Bomber Command
Aircraft factories

Despatch fighters to engage large enemy formations over land or within gliding distance of the coast. During the next two or three weeks we cannot afford to lose pilots through forced landings in the sea.

Instructions to fighter controllers, from
Air Vice-Marshal Keith Park, 19 August

RAF commanders were particularly concerned about the loss of senior pilots. Replacements were not of the same level of experience as those being shot down.

Losses

	AIRCRAFT	AIRCREW (KILLED)
Luftwaffe	328	531
Fighter Command	152	58

The collapse of Britain in the year 1940 is under present circumstances no longer to be reckoned on.
Hitler to HQ staff, 20 August

Third Phase (24 August– 6 September)

Had Göring carried on for another week or ten days hammering my fighter airfields he might have had them out of action and we could have lost the battle.
Air Vice-Marshal Keith Park, speaking in 1961

On 24 August, after a spell of bad weather, the Luftwaffe began the next phase of major raids. The main assault was against RAF sector airfields, particularly those of 11 Group. The Luftwaffe loss rate was lessening: their bombers were being escorted by large numbers of fighters and the vulnerable Stukas were no longer involved. RAF squadrons being moved into the front line suffered heavily, as they followed old tactics and weren't experienced enough. On the first night of this phase, a night-time air raid was to have major consequences.

NOTABLE DAYS OF THE BATTLE: 24 AUGUST

There were six large-scale raids, with some of the bombers forcing their way to the 11 Group stations north-east of London, at Hornchurch and North Weald.

During the raids, 12 Group were asked to provide cover for these two airfields but only one squadron arrived: 19 Squadron, its Spitfires armed with unreliable cannons.

12,000–24,000 Feet

The first Luftwaffe raid of the day was stepped in altitudes from 12,000 to 24,000 feet, presenting a difficult challenge for the defending fighters.

RAF Manston

After more raids, Manston in Kent was abandoned from this day on as a forward operating base and was only to be used for emergency landings and refuelling. Its coastal position had made it vulnerable to surprise attack. Unexploded bombs lay all over the airfield and at one point airmen had refused to come out from their air-raid shelter.

104

Number of civilians killed in a raid on Portsmouth.

Bombs on London

During a night raid German bombers missed their intended targets of the oil storage facility at Thames

Haven and the Shorts aircraft factory at Rochester. Their bombs fell on central London – the first time it had been hit. Nine people were killed and 50 injured. Göring threatened the crews responsible with demotion to the infantry; Churchill ordered reprisal raids on Berlin.

Losses

	AIRCRAFT	AIRCREW (KILLED)
Luftwaffe	41	46
Fighter Command	20	10

81

Number of RAF bombers that attacked Berlin on 25 August, in retaliation for the previous day's bombing of London. Although damage caused was not major it was an embarrassment for Göring, who had promised no RAF aircraft would fly over the German capital.

8

Number of fighter squadrons that broke up a raid on Portsmouth on 26 August.

50 TO 1

Pilot Officer Bob Doe of 234 Squadron attacked 50 Me 109s on his own on 26 August. Despite his Spitfire's engine constantly cutting out he chased one towards France before shooting it down.

THE GUNNER

At Rochford on 26 August a visiting Medical Officer went to help the crew of a Dornier that had crash-landed. As he tended to the pilot he was aware of one of the aircraft's machine guns being pointed at him by one of the crew. The RAF officer moved away quickly out of aim; he went around the fuselage, where he found the gunner had been dead the whole time. On this day the Luftwaffe lost 44 aircrew, over six times that of Fighter Command.

150

Number of German planes that bombed Liverpool on 28 August. This night-time raid followed a day's fighting during which the airfields at Rochford and Eastchurch had been hit. The Luftwaffe again lost more than 40 airmen, against Fighter Command's ten.

500 MESSERSCHMITTS

On 29 August over 500 Me 109s accompanied a much smaller number of bombers. The German's plan was to entice the RAF into committing to large dogfights but 11 Group's commander Keith Park kept his fighters away as much as possible.

NOTABLE DAYS OF THE BATTLE: 30 AUGUST

The Luftwaffe employed a new tactic, where successive attacks left little time for the RAF to regroup. The sector station at Biggin Hill was subjected to intensive bombing; Kenley was also hit. As 11 Group's aircraft were fully committed, 12 Group were asked to defend its southern neighbours' airfields; however, bombers got through and the raids continued through the afternoon with no let-up. Power lines to seven radar sites were destroyed, leaving a gap in the defences. The evening saw no reduction in the Luftwaffe's effort.

39

Number killed inside a Biggin Hill air-raid shelter. A WAAF shelter was also hit; all but one of those trapped inside were eventually dug out alive.

1,054

Sorties flown by Fighter Command – the first time it had reached four figures.

87

Bullet holes in 'Ginger' Lacey's Hurricane. He made a successful forced landing after being hit over the Thames Estuary.

SPICE AND WALLIS

Butcher's shop in Old Caterham where the operations room of RAF Kenley was moved as part of a dispersal plan.

175, 120, 75 AND 60 YARDS

Distances from which Wing Commander Tom Gleave shot down 4 Me 109s.

6

Number of aircraft lost from 222 Squadron. Three pilots were killed. It had been moved to the front line the previous day.

Losses

	AIRCRAFT	AIRCREW (KILLED)
Luftwaffe	40	57
Fighter Command	25	9

I think the death of one experienced pilot was a bigger loss to a squadron in those days than ten Spitfires or Hurricanes.
Flight Lieutenant David M. Crook, 609 Squadron

NOTABLE DAYS OF THE BATTLE: 31 AUGUST

The attacks continued with the Luftwaffe achieving an increased level of success; the RAF was under severe strain.

AIRFIELDS ATTACKED

Biggin Hill (twice)
Debden
North Weald
Detling
Hornchurch (twice)
Eastchurch
Croydon
Duxford

*Turning in the cockpit I saw the rest of the squadron
emerging from a vast eruption of smoke and debris.*

Squadron Leader Peter Townsend, 85 Squadron,
on taking off during a raid on Croydon

BIGGIN HILL FACILITIES DAMAGED OR DESTROYED

Air-raid shelters	Meteorological office
Armoury	NAAFI
Barracks	Officers' Mess
Cookhouse	Operations room
Electricity supply	Sergeants' Mess
Gas pipeline	Telephone lines
Guardroom	WAAF quarters
Hangars	Water supply
Married quarters	Workshops

After the attack, its operations room was temporarily
set up in a shop in the nearby village, before being
installed in a Victorian mansion.

DEMOLITION MAN

Biggin Hill station commander Group Captain Richard
Grice thought the Germans would continue their efforts
to destroy any buildings left standing and so he ordered
the complete demolition of the airfield's hangars. He
was court martialled but cleared.

Biggin Hill Women

During an intensive enemy air raid on an aerodrome, Sergeants Mortimer and Turner and Corporal Henderson remained at their posts and calmly carried out their duties. They displayed courage and example of a high order.
Medal citation, *The London Gazette*, 5 November

Of the six Military Medals awarded to WAAF members during the war, three were awarded to these women based at Biggin Hill:

Sergeant Joan Mortimer
Sergeant Helen Turner
Corporal Elspeth Henderson

The women helped dig victims out of bombed air-raid shelters and Sergeant Mortimer went out to the airfield's landing grounds to mark unexploded bombs with red flags to warn incoming fighters. Another WAAF to be recognised for her actions at Biggin Hill was Assistant Section Officer Felicity Hanbury. Her calm behaviour and inspiring leadership earned her the MBE.

5

Number of confirmed kills by Brian Carbury of 603 Squadron.

Losses

	AIRCRAFT	AIRCREW (KILLED)
Luftwaffe	39	21
Fighter Command	41	9

In terms of aircraft lost, this was the RAF's worst day of the battle.

EARLY SEPTEMBER

As a new month began, Fighter Command remained under pressure, its airfields being subjected to heavy attacks, reflected in its losses in the first six days:

DATE	AIRCRAFT	AIRCREW (KILLED)
1	13	6
2	14	4
3	15	6
4	17	12
5	20	8
6	20	7
TOTAL	99	43

However, they were still inflicting heavy losses on the Luftwaffe, which lost 161 aircraft and 163 airmen over the same period.

16

Average number of operational pilots per RAF fighter squadron in first week of September; 26 was the required complement.

RICHARD HILLARY

Before taking off on 3 September, 603 Squadron pilot Richard Hillary had been concerned about his cockpit canopy not sliding back quickly enough and when his aircraft was hit and caught fire, he struggled to get out. He was horribly burnt and spent months in rehabilitation. During his recovery he wrote an account of his experiences called *The Last Enemy*. He returned to flying duties but was killed in a flying accident in 1943.

4 DAYS

Length of time the Vickers aircraft factory at Brooklands was out of action after being bombed again on 4 September. As Germany's commanders planned for a switch in strategy, the Luftwaffe continued their attacks on aircraft factories and airfields.

AIRCRAFT SUPPLY

During this third phase of the battle, Fighter Command faced a deficit in supply. Like the pilots, the workers were exhausted from their efforts during the summer.

Aircraft damaged and destroyed	466
Replacements	269

Dowding even considered moving his aircraft back from the front line, out of the range of the bombers.

AIRFIELD ATTACKS

Major attacks on Fighter Command airfields between 12 August and 6 September:

Biggin Hill	11	West Malling	2
Manston	6	Rochford	2
Hornchurch	5	Middle Wallop	2
Lympne	4	Kenley	2
North Weald	3	Warmwell	1
Hawkinge	3	Tangmere	1
Debden	3	Martlesham Heath	1
Croydon	3	Gravesend	1

In this phase, six of 11 Group's seven sector stations were badly damaged.

Losses

	AIRCRAFT	AIRCREW (KILLED)
Luftwaffe	413	454
Fighter Command	264	106

In England they're filled with curiosity and keep asking, 'Why doesn't he come?' Be calm. Be calm. He's coming. He's coming!
Adolf Hitler, Berlin, 4 September

Fourth Phase
(7–30 September)

---

*And should the Royal Air Force declare that they will
attack our cities on a large scale, we will erase theirs!*
Adolf Hitler, Berlin, 4 September

It must be realised that we are going downhill.
Air Chief Marshal Dowding to Air Vice-Marshal
Douglas, Deputy Chief of the Air Staff, 7 September

Despite the drafting in of pilots from Bomber and
Coastal Commands, there was still a shortage of trained
and effective pilots, but Keith Park believed the RAF
would be able to withstand its losses longer than the
Luftwaffe. Despite claims by Generalfeldmarschall
Kesselring that the RAF was on its last legs on 6
September, Fighter Command still had more than 750
fighters and 1,300 pilots available for action.

NOTABLE DAYS OF THE BATTLE: 7 SEPTEMBER

*There were so many enemy fighters layered
up to 30,000 feet that it was just like looking
up the escalator at Piccadilly Circus.*
Unnamed Spitfire pilot

Three waves attacked in an aerial armada, whose size shocked the RAF pilots rising to meet it. The RAF controllers were deceived into thinking the formations would split into smaller groups to bomb the fighter airfields and were caught flat-footed when the German aircraft continued on to the capital. Hitler hoped the attacks would force Churchill's government to fall and be replaced by one seeking peace; Göring thought that the RAF would have to defend the capital and so would come up to battle where it could be defeated, in the air. The target was east London's docklands and many of the bombers got through. The attacks carried on into the evening with the fires acting as target indicators. The Blitz, which would last until May 1941, had begun.

348

Number of Luftwaffe bombers in the first wave, plotted at 3.54 p.m.

617

Numbers of escorting fighters for the first wave.

23

Number of RAF squadrons sent to meet the first wave.

40 RODING ROAD, LOUGHTON, ESSEX

When Hurricane R4173 was shot down its pilot parachuted to safety, but the aircraft crashed into the back garden of 40 Roding Road, killing three people in their air-raid shelter.

> *These raids created a lot of damage in London. The provisional casualty list says 400 dead and 1,500 seriously injured. What complete swines these Jerries are.*
>
> Pilot Officer Denis Wissler, diary entry 7 September
> (he was shot down and killed on 11 November)

436

Number of Londoners killed; 1,600 were badly injured.

Losses

	AIRCRAFT	AIRCREW (KILLED)
Luftwaffe	41	52
Fighter Command	25	16

STABILISATION SCHEME

With no fresh squadrons ready to be brought into the front line, on 8 September Dowding introduced a categorisation scheme:

SQUADRON CATEGORY	DETAILS
A	Squadrons in 11 Group and at Duxford and Middle Wallop were to be kept at full strength.
B	Remaining 10 & 12 Group squadrons to be kept at full strength, to relieve 'A' squadrons.
C	Experienced pilots to be moved to 'A' squadrons, leaving 5 or 6 of them behind to train novice flyers.

SINGLE SQUADRON VERSUS 'BIG WING'

	SQUADRON ATTACKS	BIG WING
Advocates:	Park/Dowding	Leigh-Mallory/Bader
Method:	Single squadron attacks	Several squadrons (up to five)
Tactics:	Squadrons would attack formations as soon as possible.	Squadrons would gather and attack together.

Strategic Aims:	Theory was if the defences were maintained intact the Germans would eventually give up, having not achieved their aims.	It was hoped the Germans would abandon their offensive due to high losses.
Advantages:	The fighters would get to the bombers before they reached their targets. Not all aircraft would be on the ground refuelling and rearming at the same time. More raids could be attacked at one time.	They would be able to destroy more enemy aircraft at one time.
Disadvantages:	The fighters were often outnumbered.	Took time to assemble the formations. Was only suitable for certain occasions, e.g. when large formations attacked London. Meant attacking after the bombers had dropped their bombs.

The 'Big Wing' formation of several squadrons was first used in action on 7 September, with limited success, but it was one of the most divisive aspects of the RAF's running of the war. The debate was between 11 and 12 Group commanders over how best to meet the incoming Luftwaffe.

11 Group's Keith Park had been disappointed when 12 Group's fighters either arrived late or not at all when asked to defend his airfields. Park's disappointment with 12 Group was contrasted with his satisfaction with 10 Group, who sent aircraft when requested.

> *Had I adopted Bader's Big Wing*
> *I would have lost the battle.*
> Air Vice-Marshal Keith Park, speaking in 1961

INVASION FEARS

> *We cannot tell when they will try to come; we cannot*
> *be sure that in fact they will try at all; but no one*
> *should blind himself to the fact that a heavy, full-*
> *scale invasion of this island is being prepared with*
> *all the usual German thoroughness and method.*
> Winston Churchill, 11 September

Fear of invasion was widespread in the summer of 1940, coming to a head in early September. Throughout the summer RAF photo-reconnaissance aircraft had reported the build-up of vessels in the Channel ports, and the bombing of London on 7 September was taken as an indicator of an imminent invasion.

If the Germans come by parachute, aeroplane or ship,
you must remain where you are. The order is 'stay put'.

Extract from pamphlet entitled 'If the Invader
Comes. What to do – and how to do it.'

'CROMWELL'

Code word for British Army home defence troops and
the Home Guard to move from 8-hours readiness to
immediate notice. Its issuing on 7 September was
misinterpreted as meaning the invasion was actually
taking place and panic arose in some areas.

DEFENCES

By September defences were well advanced around the
British coast. They took many forms:

Anti-glider poles – erected in fields or flat areas
  thought to be potential landing sites
Anti-tank barriers (including cubes, cylinders and
  'dragon's teeth')
Anti-tank ditches
Barbed wire
Beach scaffolding – intended to stop boats and tanks
Bridges armed with demolition charges
Coastal gun batteries
Flame traps – oil would be released from concealed oil
  tanks and ignited when a German tank passed over it
Minefields

Pillboxes – these concrete or brick, round or hexagonal defensive posts could house infantry or artillery

Roadblocks (including the 'hedgehog' and 'hairpin' metal barriers that used lengths of railway track)

New Tactics

On 11 September, Park ordered that squadrons should be sent in pairs to combine their firepower, with Spitfires targeting high-flying Me 109 escorts and Hurricanes attacking bombers and close escorts. He also demanded fighters keep to the altitude they were given for the bombers, as it was common for sector controllers and squadron commanders to add a few thousand feet on to ensure the fighters were above their targets, which led to some bombers being missed.

The Battle Continues

The second week of September saw a mixture of poor weather and smaller-scale day raids, but with the night-time bombing of cities continuing around the country.

DATE	DETAILS
8	Light day raids, with the RAF flying less than half the sorties of the previous day.
9	Luftwaffe mounted large raids but were surprised to be met with determined resistance. RAF fighters prevented most of the bombers getting through.

10	Bad weather prevented large raids until night. A large fire consumed St Katherine's Dock in London.
11	Two waves in the afternoon headed to London and were met by large numbers of defenders, who suffered more losses than the attackers on this occasion.
12	Poor weather meant few Luftwaffe bombers ventured across the Channel.
13	Bad weather. Small raids – some featuring single bombers – were carried out during the day.
14	Poor weather again, but some raids were launched in the morning against radar stations. This allowed a gap through which bombers got to Eastbourne and Brighton. In the afternoon, bigger raids on London were attempted but the weather hadn't improved and accuracy was poor. One raid was met by ten squadrons of fighters and turned back. Despite this, Fighter Command's responses were uncoordinated, which led to the Luftwaffe believing it was failing.

*I'm glad we've been bombed. It makes me
feel I can look the East End in the face.*

Queen Elizabeth after Buckingham Palace
was bombed on 13 September

NOTABLE DAYS OF THE BATTLE: 15 SEPTEMBER

In the week since the first raid on London, the RAF had been able to rest and replenish. In two waves, the Luftwaffe mounted a large day raid on London on what they hoped would be a decisive day. There were no feints used and the Luftwaffe was met by RAF fighters, who attacked all the way in and then again as the Luftwaffe was on the way out. It was a successful day for the RAF, but there was a feeling it should have brought down more German aircraft, with the bombers particularly vulnerable, having flown much of the time over Britain unescorted (their fighter escorts were low on fuel and had turned back).

AREAS OF LONDON BOMBED (FIRST WAVE)

Battersea	Lambeth
Beckenham	Lewisham
Camberwell	Tooting
Clapham	Wandsworth
Crystal Palace	Westminster

There are none.

Keith Park's response to Churchill's enquiry on his reserves.

BIG WING

Big Wing aircraft that attacked the first wave	55
Luftwaffe aircraft shot down	5
Big Wing losses	6

*Pilot attacked a Dornier 17 from astern and soon
silenced the rear gunner. The enemy aircraft dived
into the clouds with white smoke pouring from
both engines. The pilot followed it through the
clouds and saw it crash on the top of a house.*
Combat report by Pilot Officer W. K. Stansfield, 242 Squadron

Losses

	AIRCRAFT	AIRCREW (KILLED)
Luftwaffe	61	93
Fighter Command	31	16

As they limped home, Luftwaffe crews realised
that Göring's statement that the RAF was down to
its last 50 Spitfires was far from the truth.

*175 Raiders Shot Down
A Great Air Battle
Half Enemy Force Destroyed
RAF Batter Invasion Machine*
Headlines from *The Times*, 16 September

LUFTWAFFE TACTICS

On 16 September Göring ordered that, for day raids,
small numbers of bombers were to be escorted by large

numbers of fighters. He also claimed, not for the first time, that Fighter Command would soon be destroyed.

177

Number of operational aircraft the Luftwaffe thought Fighter Command had on 16 September. In reality it had over 600 operational fighters, with over 200 in reserve. The Luftwaffe had underestimated British aircraft manufacturing and overestimated its pilots' combat claims.

Gieves Limited
Late 21 Old Bond Street W1
Are Carrying On
at 80 Piccadilly W1.
Customers are asked to extend their
forbearance for two days.
Gieves send respectful greetings to the Services with
the assurance that they will not let them down.
Notice in *The Times*, 20 September

The well-known military tailor's premises suffered a direct hit on the evening of 16 September. The 'business as usual' attitude, while not adopted by all the population, was a feature that gave rise to the 'Blitz spirit'.

Invasion Cancellation

On 17 September Hitler called off the invasion as conditions had not been met. However, preparations for invasion were continued 'solely for the purpose of maintaining political and military pressure on Britain'. Operation Sea Lion preparations also helped obscure the build-up for the summer 1941 invasion of the Soviet Union. Hitler had told his commanders in August to begin preparing plans for what would be Operation Barbarossa.

If Russia is crushed, Britain's last hopes will have gone.
Adolf Hitler, 31 July

On the water we were utterly defenceless and it would have ended in disaster. In the long talks amongst us soldiers the opinion emerged that this was nothing but a suicide mission.
Wilhelm Küchle, German soldier, speaking of Operation Sea Lion in 1998

7.30 P.M. TO 5.30 A.M.

Duration of night bombing on night of 18/19 September. London and Liverpool bore the brunt of the attacks.

70

Number of solo Luftwaffe aircraft that crossed the Channel on 19 September. Ten were shot down. No

Fighter Command aircraft were lost – the first day this had happened in 7 weeks.

'I'M ALL RIGHT, OLD PAL, DUTCHY CAN TAKE IT'

Last words of Pilot Officer Dennis 'Dutch' Holland after being admitted to hospital on 20 September. He died of his wounds later that day.

158

Sorties flown by Fighter Command on 22 September – the lowest number since the battle began.

10 MILES

Width of Luftwaffe formation on the morning of 24 September. It was turned back from reaching London by fierce resistance. A later wave of attacks was just as big.

0

Number of fighter squadrons that engaged the second wave. The raiders attacked at low level and were able to avoid being detected. Only anti-aircraft fire provided resistance, bringing down several bombers.

Aircraft Factory Attacks

DATE	FACTORY	LOCATION	RESULTS
21	Hawker	Weybridge, Surrey	Little damage
24	Supermarine	Woolston, Southampton	Little damage, but 100 killed in a bombed shelter
25	Bristol	Filton, Bristol	Production interrupted, 250 killed or injured
26	Supermarine	Woolston and Itchen, Southampton	Production halted, 30 killed

35

Number of dispersed sites the production of Spitfires was moved to following the bombing of the factories at Woolston and Itchen. Spitfires were built in garages, bus stations and a laundry.

NOTABLE DAYS OF THE BATTLE: 27 SEPTEMBER

In spite of the heavy losses we are inflicting on the enemy fighters, no decisive decrease in their number or fighting efficiency was noticeable.
Adolf Galland to Hermann Göring, 27 September

The aircraft factory at Filton was to be attacked but the planes were intercepted before they could bomb the target. A force of Me 110 fighter-bombers, escorted by Me 109s, was attacked all the way across the south-east of England towards London, as wave after wave of bombers were turned back. A bad day for the Luftwaffe saw it suffer double the RAF's aircraft losses and four times the aircrew.

BATTLE OF GRAVENEY MARSH

This 'battle' was the only one fought on British soil during the war. When a German Junkers Ju 88 crash-landed, its crew armed themselves and shot at approaching troops. Shots were exchanged until the German airmen eventually surrendered.

177,000

Number of people who took to the London Underground on the night of 27 September. The authorities were initially not keen on them being used as shelters but bowed to public pressure.

Losses

	AIRCRAFT	AIRCREW (KILLED)
Luftwaffe	57	81
Fighter Command	28	20

1,173

Number of daytime sorties flown by Fighter Command on 30 September – its highest total of the battle. Two raids on London were turned back after a hard day's fighting. The RAF inflicted heavy losses on the Luftwaffe's last large daylight raid.

Losses

	AIRCRAFT	AIRCREW (KILLED)
Luftwaffe	47	59
Fighter Command	21	8

Fourth Phase Losses (7–30 September)

	AIRCRAFT	AIRCREW (KILLED)
Luftwaffe	468	666
Fighter Command	259	130

Fifth Phase
(1–31 October)

Due to losses suffered, daylight bombing by large formations of Heinkels, Dorniers and Junkers was halted, and they were switched to night bombing. Smaller-scale raids by Junkers Ju 88s and heavily escorted Me 109 and 110 fighter-bombers took over during the day.

'MESSERSCHMITT MONTH'

Term used by RAF pilots to describe October 1940 due to the frequency of raids featuring those German fighters.

NUMBER OF SERVICEABLE ME 109s

| 1 July | 725 |
| 1 October | 275 |

The Luftwaffe was not able to resupply its front-line fighter units as the RAF had done and single-seat fighters were at a premium. The situation had not been helped when a third were assigned fighter-bomber roles in September.

'JABO'

Short for Jagdbomber, this was the fighter-bomber version of the Me 109. Pilots were given rudimentary training in how to drop bombs, with many resenting being diverted from their role as pure fighter pilots. These fighter-bombers were not hugely effective, but they were not easy to intercept and did cause problems for the defences. They would fly at 30,000 feet where radar couldn't detect them effectively. In response, the RAF mounted standing patrols which resulted in tired pilots flying long hours.

550 POUNDS

Weight of bombs carried by each Me 109 'Jabo'.

NIGHT DEFENCE

Luftwaffe night bombers suffered few combat losses. The RAF had no effective night fighters and its inability to shoot down night raiders was held against Dowding. It would not be until 1941 that Fighter Command would have useful night fighters equipped with airborne radar.

17

Number of day-bombing formations launched against Britain on 2 October. Aircraft in the formations numbered from one to over 50.

3½ Feet (1 Metre)

Length of wingtip knocked off the Hurricane flown by Pilot Officer Ken Mackenzie of 501 Squadron on 7 October. Having run out of ammunition while attacking a Messerschmitt 109, Mackenzie destroyed the German fighter's left-hand tailplane with his starboard wing. He was awarded the Distinguished Flying Cross for his actions.

Sorties

As the month went on, fatigue became a concern amongst pilots, seen by the number of sorties flown in one week.

DATE	FIGHTER COMMAND SORTIES
7	825
8	639
9	400+
10	754
11	949
12	797
13	591

'The Devil Looks After His Own'

Comment by a Labour MP following the destruction of the Conservative Party's Carlton Club on 14 October. All the club's staff and members survived unhurt. Five hundred Londoners were killed in the attacks that same night.

15

Number of waves of 'Jabos' that attacked on 15 October. Most headed for London, the main target of the fighter-bombers.

2,633

Number of 'Jabo' sorties flown against London in October.

3.40 P.M.

In May 2014 a watch was put up for auction, formerly owned by Flying Officer Les Ricalton of 74 Squadron. Ricalton was shot down on 17 October over Kent and the watch he was wearing stopped at the time he was hit: 3.40 p.m.

90

Sorties flown by Fighter Command on 23 October – the lowest of the entire battle. The battle was drifting to an end.

0

Number of RAF aircraft shot down by Italy's air force, the Corpo Aereo Italiano. Mussolini was keen on his air force taking part in the attacks on Britain and Italian bombers and fighters were sent to operate from bases in Belgium in the last week of the battle. They suffered heavy losses due to flying in adverse weather they were not used to and their aircraft were not as capable as others. They were still using biplane fighters.

0

Number of aircraft lost by both sides on the last official day of the battle.

Fifth Phase Losses (1–31 October)

	AIRCRAFT	AIRCREW (KILLED)
Luftwaffe	379	492
Fighter Command	185	120

While we are predominant at sea and until Germany has defeated our fighter forces, invasion by sea is not a practical operation of war.

Admiral of the Fleet Sir Charles Forbes, to War Cabinet Defence Committee, 31 October

Aftermath

Fighter Command's pilots were never required to mount such intensive defensive sorties again. Night fighters continued to tackle the Luftwaffe during the Blitz but the numbers involved were much smaller. After May 1941, air raids on Britain lessened as aircraft were moved in preparation for the invasion of the USSR.

From 1941 onwards British-based fighters were used in a similar way as Luftwaffe Me 109s had been in 1940: crossing the Channel to harass the air defences and encourage the defending aircraft to rise to meet them. These 'Rhubarb' and 'Circus' missions were costly – Douglas Bader was shot down on one – and their effectiveness was questioned.

Fighter Boys

Fighter Command's pilots were seen as flamboyant exponents of Britain's armed forces, but behind the smiling, devil-may-care image lay the reality of battle-hardened military personnel who faced risk on a daily basis.

18

Geoffrey Wellum's age when he joined 92 Squadron in May 1940. Nicknamed 'Boy', he flew throughout the battle and went on to a post-war career in the RAF, leaving military service in 1961.

TOP BUTTON

Fighter pilots made themselves stand out from other RAF aircrew by leaving the top button of their uniforms undone.

MILLIONAIRES' MOB

Nickname for 601 (County of London) Squadron. 601 was an Auxiliary Air Force unit known to be exclusive in its pre-war membership. When worried about fuel supplies for their private cars one member, William Rhodes-Moorhouse, bought a garage.

NAMES GIVEN TO AIRCRAFT OF 603 (CITY OF EDINBURGH) SQUADRON

Aorangi
Ard Choille
Auld Reekie
Blue Peter
Excalibur
Hell
Sredni Vashtar
Tigger

NICKNAMES

Many pilots were given nicknames for a variety of reasons, from puns to reflections of their character:

Ace	Bubble	Cocky	Fanny
Arty	Buck	Colt	Farmer
Bear	Bunny	Crow	Ginger
Bolster	Buzz	Dogs	Grubby
Broody	Cobber	Dutch	Grumpy

Hank	Polly	Sheep	Unlucky
Hilly	Popper	Shovel	Watty
Jumbo	Prof	Stapme	Weasel
Mitch	Razz	Taffy	Widge
Mouse	Rubber	Tannoy	Wombat
Pancho	Rusty	Teddy	Wonky
Pinker	Sammy	Tubby	
Pip	Sandy	Uncle	

NATIONALITIES

Although Churchill spoke of 'the Few', almost 3,000 men flew with Fighter Command during the battle. The bulk of them were British, but a fifth of those who came to Britain to fly and fight were nationals of another country:

Australia	32
Belgium	28
Canada	112
Czechoslovakia	89
France	13
Great Britain	2,340
Ireland	10
Jamaica	1
New Zealand	127
Poland	145
Rhodesia	3
South Africa	25
USA	9
Total:	2,934

FOREIGN SQUADRONS

*Had it not been for the magnificent material
contributed by the Polish squadrons and their
unsurpassed gallantry, I hesitate to say that the
outcome of the Battle would have been the same.*
Air Chief Marshal Hugh Dowding

While most flew within regular RAF squadrons some of
the nationalities were given distinct units:

NATIONALITY	SQUADRON	NOTES
Polish	302, 303	The Polish pilots were combat-experienced following their country's 1939 invasion by Germany. The RAF were initially unsure of their abilities but after a Polish pilot shot down a Dornier on 30 August when on a training mission, they were sent to the front line.
Czech	310, 312	After the war both squadrons became part of the re-formed Czech Air Force. The second-highest scoring RAF pilot of the battle was Czech Josef František, who actually flew with the Polish 303 Squadron.

Canadian	1 (Canadian)	The squadron brought its own Hurricanes over from Canada. Douglas Bader's 242 Squadron also had a large contingent of Canadian pilots.

126

Number of aircraft shot down in 42 days by 303 Squadron, the RAF's highest-scoring squadron.

4 FEET 10 INCHES (1.47 M)

Height of Vernon 'Shorty' Keogh, the shortest RAF pilot of the war. Keogh, an American who, along with several compatriots, disobeyed their country's neutrality orders to fly with the RAF, used two cushions to see out of the cockpit. He later joined the American-only 71 'Eagle' Squadron. Keogh was killed on operations in February 1941.

Life on a Squadron

Don't come and tell. Ring this like HELL!
Message chalked onto squadron dispersal bell

A fighter squadron's typical day would see pilots up early to be ready for first light. Aircraft were dispersed around the airfield, where they were harder to hit than they would be gathered together in large hangars. The machines would have their engines warmed up and the pilot's guns, oxygen and other equipment would be checked, ready for immediate action. The pilots would then sit and wait. They could relax if the weather was poor but if it was fine they would remain near their fighters all day awaiting a scramble order. The Luftwaffe pilots' experiences were similar but differed in one crucial respect: they knew when they would be ordered into action.

FOOD

It was rarely possible for pilots to have time to go to the station's mess for meals and so food was brought out to them. At RAF Warmwell the station commander banned one squadron's pilots from using the kitchens when they cooked their own breakfast after the civilian kitchen staff had refused to get up early. The squadron resorted to bringing in camping equipment.

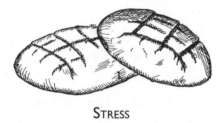

STRESS

Pilots led a life divided between being relatively comfortable on the ground to being quickly engaged in the maelstrom of aerial combat. The situation of being suddenly called into action caused high levels of stress: RAF ace 'Ginger' Lacey was sick before each take-off and pilots would be startled whenever the duty telephone rang.

KANALKRANKHEIT (CHANNEL SICKNESS)

As the battle wore on German pilots also began to show signs of combat-related stress, with symptoms such as stomach pains, appetite loss, nausea and shortness of temper. Some would feign illness or report spurious aircraft malfunctions to avoid flying. Doctors diagnosed appendicitis in order for the men to have several weeks' break.

FATIGUE

Pilots of both sides constantly battled tiredness. The long summer days meant missions continued for longer and the hours available for sleep were limited. One pilot at 54 Squadron fell asleep at the dinner table, landing face-first in his eggs and bacon. Another pilot dozed off while taxying in his Hurricane.

BUSY SCHEDULE

7.00 a.m.
8.40 a.m.
10.20 a.m.
12.00 p.m.
1.40 p.m.
3.20 p.m.
5.00 p.m.

Take-off times flown by Messerschmitt pilot Ulrich Steinhilper over one day. With the heavy demands on them, Luftwaffe fighter pilots were afforded few periods of rest.

RECREATION

Despite pilots being tired, many still made time to visit the local pubs to unwind. Hangovers were cured by adrenalin and the oxygen from the pilots' masks.

PUB	NEARBY AIRFIELD
The Old Jail	Biggin Hill
The White Hart	Biggin Hill
The Red Lion	Duxford
The Plough	Duxford
Chequers	Fowlmere
The Black Swan ('Mucky Duck')	Middle Wallop
The Orchard	Northolt
The Ship	Tangmere
The Dolphin	Tangmere
The Square Club	Warmwell

ROTATION

Fighter Command squadrons that had suffered heavy losses would be moved out of the front line to recuperate and rebuild. For example, 145 Squadron lost 11 pilots in a month and was transferred to Drem in East Lothian. Luftwaffe crews were not rested in the same way.

Ground Crew

Ground crew were vital. They prepared the fighters before combat, and then refuelled and rearmed them afterwards. They also repaired damaged machines, commonly working through the night. A three-man ground-crew team looked after each RAF aircraft. Each had their own responsibilities:

Fitter	Engine
Rigger	Airframe, undercarriage
Armourer	Machine guns, ammunition

Turnaround Time

Time was critical between sorties and much effort was made to ready the fighters for combat as quickly as possible:

Spitfire	26 minutes
Hurricane	9 minutes

The Spitfire took longer to turn around because its gun positions were more complicated to service.

Shortage

We were short of pilots from early in the battle.
Air Vice-Marshal Keith Park

While the British supply of aircraft was maintained, that of aircrew was under strain through vital parts of the battle.

58

Number of Royal Navy pilots transferred to Fighter Command. Eighteen were subsequently killed.

2 Weeks

Length of time trainee fighter pilots would spend at an Operational Training Unit before being transferred to a front-line squadron. The course was previously delivered over six weeks, but in mid August the need for pilots saw them moved more speedily. Novice flyers were at an increased risk of being shot down; many were lost on their first sortie.

I was very ill equipped to fly in combat, and the results proved it. People like me were joining and being shot out of the sky in seconds because we just didn't know what it was all about.
Sergeant Pilot Bill Green, 501 Squadron

Gunnery

Pilots arrived at squadrons with little in the way of gunnery practice. Some had never fired an aircraft's guns until in combat.

Surviving the Battle

I received no fighter training whatsoever.
The first time I saw a Hurricane was when
I arrived at Biggin Hill in July 1940.
Sergeant Pilot Tony Pickering, 501 Squadron

4 OUT OF 5

Proportion of pilots shot down who were unaware of their attacker.

If Chicago gangsters can have bulletproof
glass in their cars I can't see any reason why
my pilots should not have the same.
Air Chief Marshal Hugh Dowding

Dowding's request was met with laughter but he refused to give up and eventually Triplex was fitted to the fighters' front windscreens.

DITCHING

When ditching in the sea, both the Spitfire and the Hurricane would quickly tip over as the underwing radiators scooped up water. This reduced the time to escape before the aircraft sank.

'MAE WEST'

Nickname for RAF life jackets, stemming from the physique of the Hollywood entertainer.

4 HOURS

Time a pilot could survive in the English Channel before succumbing to hypothermia. Unlike the Germans, the RAF didn't have an established air-sea rescue service and pilots weren't issued with dinghies.

I was bloody glad to feel that boat hook up my arse!
Pilot Officer E. Farnes, 141 Squadron

On 19 July Farnes had baled out of his stricken Defiant. As the aircraft's gunner, he was equipped with special flying clothing, which unfortunately positioned him face down in the water.

RED CROSS SEAPLANES

The German Heinkel 59 seaplanes were painted white with red crosses on their wings and fuselage. The British Air Ministry issued an order in July that these aircraft were to be shot down, as they were thought to be carrying out reconnaissance and were therefore legitimate targets. The Germans were infuriated at what they regarded as a war crime.

LOBSTER POTS

British nickname for anchored buoys positioned by the Germans for any of their airmen that had baled out into the sea. They were large enough to house rations and first aid kit, and even bunks for one or more airmen. Both sides used them, and not just humans: seals were also spotted having moved in.

80 PER CENT

Estimated percentage of RAF aircrew who were not rescued after landing in the Channel.

HANDGUNS

As in the First World War, some aircrew – of both sides – carried handguns in case they became trapped and chose to take a quick 'exit'. Luftwaffe commanders later banned crews from carrying them.

'BOBBING'

Method of mixing gliding with short periods of powered climbing, used to fly aircraft low on fuel or damaged back across the Channel. Named after Messerschmitt 109 pilot Hans-Ekkehard Bob, who used the technique to make it back to France.

One unfortunate German rear-gunner baled out of the Dornier 17 I attacked, but his parachute caught on the tail. There he was, swinging helplessly, with the aircraft swooping and diving and staggering all over the sky, being pulled about by the man hanging by his parachute from the tail. That bomber went crashing into the Thames estuary, with the swinging gunner still there.

Unidentified Hurricane pilot, in wartime RAF publication *We Speak from the Air*

AL DEERE'S NINE LIVES

Spitfire pilot Al Deere entitled his memoir *Nine Lives* due to the close escapes he had in his flying career. Five of his 'lives' were used up during three months of the battle:

DATE	DETAILS	INJURIES SUSTAINED
11 July	Collided with Me 109, crash-landed.	Various
15 August	Shot down by Luftwaffe, taken to hospital.	Fractured wrist
28 August	Shot down by Spitfire, baled out.	Uninjured
31 August	During an air raid, aircraft blown upside down by bomb while taking off. Travelled 100 yards before stopping.	Head and neck injuries

September	Collided with Spitfire during practice dogfight, baled out.	Back injuries

McIndoe's Army

At Queen Victoria Hospital in East Grinstead, a special unit was set up by surgeon Archibald McIndoe to care for the many burnt airmen. McIndoe introduced innovative treatments such as the use of saline baths and, recognising the psychological effects of these injuries on the young men, established an unusual environment for a hospital: singing, alcohol and open flirtation between the nursing staff and patients were all encouraged.

649

Number of members of the Guinea Pig Club, formed of McIndoe's patients, by the end of the war.

'The Town That Did Not Stare'

Name given to East Grinstead, where the men, some of whom were badly disfigured, were made to feel welcome.

15

Number of operations performed on Geoffrey Page of 56 Squadron, who was badly burnt on 12 August. He returned to operational flying three years later.

PRISONERS OF WAR

Although German airmen were generally treated well, there were occasions when they were subjected to harsh treatment. One pilot who landed off the Isle of Wight was met by a rowing boat whose occupants beat him with oars until he sank under the water. A Luftwaffe crew member who parachuted into the sea off Eastbourne was seen but left unattended.

'THE ONE WHO GOT AWAY'

Of all the German airmen captured, only one made it back: Franz von Werra, who was shot down in September 1940. He was transported to Canada, where he escaped, reaching Mexico before flying to Germany. He returned to flying duties but died when his aircraft crashed in the North Sea in October 1941.

967

Number of Luftwaffe crewmen taken prisoner between 1 July and 31 October 1940.

Facts and Figures

0

Number of days in the battle when the Luftwaffe didn't lose an aircraft. The RAF had five.

1 IN 6

Proportion of Fighter Command aircrew who were killed.

20

Average age of an RAF pilot in 1940.

40

Aircraft shot down by Luftwaffe Captain Helmut Wick, the highest-scoring pilot of the battle.

57

Number of nights of consecutive bombing on London during September and October.

71

Number of squadrons who flew in Fighter Command.

72

Weekly hours worked by staff at Derby's Rolls-Royce engine factory during peak production.

90

Time in seconds it took a well-honed squadron to have all its aircraft take off from the scramble order.

104

Number of RAF pilots who claimed to have shot down five or more enemy aircraft.

114

Duration in days of the battle.

126

Operational sorties flown by North Weald station commander Wing Commander Victor Beamish. The 37-year-old Irishman flew 31 sorties as 'self lone patrol' and claimed several kills.

175

Number of Fighter Command aircrew with no known grave.

£264

Annual salary of RAF Pilot Officer in 1940.

600

Coastal Command airmen lost in 6 months, while flying patrols over the Channel ports to look for signs of the German invasion.

791

Rounds fired by anti-aircraft guns from July to September for each Luftwaffe aircraft brought down.

801

Number of RAF Bomber Command aircrew killed.

1,578

Fighter Command airmen who flew in the battle and survived the war.

4,349,900

Number of copies sold of *The Battle of Britain* pamphlet, published in 1941. Its publication in America was part of the propaganda effort to retain American support.

Battle of Britain Losses

	AIRCRAFT	AIRCREW (KILLED)
Luftwaffe	1,887	2,662
Fighter Command	1,023	537

British Civilians Killed in Bombing Raids

July	258
August	1,075
September	6,954
October	6,334

COMMEMORATIONS

BATTLE OF BRITAIN AT HOME DAYS

In 1942, 15 September was chosen as the day when commemorations would take place. Around this date each year the RAF held 'At Home' days. The last Battle of Britain At Home airshow was held in 2013 at RAF Leuchars in Fife.

MEMORIALS

The battle and those who took part have been commemorated in many ways since 1940:

RAF Battle of Britain Memorial Flight
The Battle of Britain Monument, London
National Memorial to the Few, Capel-le-Ferne, Kent
Royal Air Force Chapel with Memorial Window, Westminster Abbey, London
Saint George's Royal Air Force Chapel of Remembrance, Biggin Hill
'Battle of Britain' Class locomotives
Keith Park statue, London
Hugh Dowding statue, London
Mortimer Road, Stowmarket
Townsend Square, West Malling
Ken Mackenzie Close, Lutterworth
Benzie Lake, Canada (named after Pilot Officer John Benzie of 242 Squadron, who was killed on 7 September)

CHURCH OF ST LAWRENCE

Each year on the anniversary of the death of Pilot Officer Lawrence Whitbread, the Church of St Lawrence in Ludlow is floodlit in his honour.

In Fadeless Memory of
Thomas Brian Kirk
Sgt Pilot 74th Squadron
RAF Biggin Hill.
Mortally wounded in action,
Battle of Britain 1940.
Died 22 July 1941
Aged 22 years.

Headstone inscription of just one of 'the Few' who died of his wounds in 1941

Sources

BOOKS

Addison, Paul & Crang, Jeremy (Editors): *The Burning Blue: A New History of the Battle of Britain*. (Pimlico, 2000)

Ansel, Walter: *Hitler Confronts England* (Duke University Press, 1960)

Brewster Daniels, Stephen: *Rescue from the Skies: The Story of the Airborne Lifeboats* (HMSO, 1993)

Bungay, Stephen: *The Most Dangerous Enemy: A History of the Battle of Britain* (Aurum Press, 2009)

Cecil, Robert: *Hitler's Decision to Invade Russia, 1941* (Davis-Poynter, 1975)

Collier, Basil: *The Defence of the United Kingdom* (HMSO, 1957)

Crook, Flt Lt David M.: *Spitfire Pilot: A Personal Account of the Battle of Britain* (Grub Street, 2008)

Deere, Alan C.: *Nine Lives* (Crecy, 1999)

Goss, Chris: *Luftwaffe Fighter-Bombers Over Britain: The Tip and Run Campaign, 1942–43* (Stackpole Books, 2010)

Grinnell-Milne, Duncan: *The Silent Victory: September 1940* (White Lion, 1976)

Hewitt, Geoff: *Hitler's Armada: The Royal Navy and the Defence of Great Britain, April–October 1940* (Pen & Sword Maritime, 2008)

Hillary, Richard: *The Last Enemy* (Pimlico, 1997)

Holland, James: *The Battle of Britain* (Bantam, 2010)

James, T. C. G.: *The Battle of Britain* (Frank Cass, 2000)

Kershaw, Alex: *The Few, July–October 1940* (Penguin, 2008)

Lavery, Brian: *Churchill's Navy: The Ships, Men and Organisation, 1939–1945* (Conway, 2008)

Mason, Francis K.: *The British Fighter since 1912* (Putnam, 1992)

Mason, Francis K.: *The Hawker Hurricane: An Illustrated History* (Crecy, 2000)

Mason, Air Vice Marshal Tony: *To Inherit the Skies: From Spitfire to Tornado* (Brassey's, 1990)

McKinstry, Leo: *Operation Sealion: How Britain Crushed the German War Machine's Dreams of Invasion in 1940* (John Murray, 2014)

Mitcham, Samuel W.: *Eagles of the Third Reich: Men of the Luftwaffe in WWII* (Stackpole Books, 2007)

Murray, Williamson: *Military Adaptation in War: With Fear of Change* (Cambridge University Press, 2011)

Overy, R. J.: *The Air War 1939–1945* (Europa Publications, 1980)

Overy, R. J.: *The Battle: Summer 1940* (Penguin, 2000)

Parker, Matthew: *The Battle of Britain, July–October 1940: An Oral History of Britain's Finest Hour* (Headline, 2000)

Price, Alfred: *Spitfire Mark I/II Aces 1939–41* (Osprey, 1996)

Price, Alfred: *The Spitfire Story* (Arms & Armour Press, 1992)

Ramsey, Winston G. (Editor): *The Battle of Britain: Then and Now* (After the Battle, 1989)

Richard, Denis: *Royal Air Force 1939–1945, Volume 1: The Fight at Odds* (HMSO, 1974)

Robinson, Derek: *Invasion, 1940* (Robinson, 2006)

Roof Over Britain. The Official Story of the A.A. Defences 1939–1942 (HMSO, 1943)

Roskill, Captain S.W.: *The War at Sea 1939–1945, Volume I: The Defensive* (HMSO, 1976)

Ross, David & Blanche, Bruce & Simpson, William: *The Greatest Squadron of Them All: The Definitive History of 603 (City of Edinburgh) Squadron RAuxAF, Volume 1* (Grub St, 2003)

Spencer Shew, Betty: *Queen Elizabeth, The Queen Mother* (Hodder & Stoughton, 1955)

Steinhilper, Ulrich & Osborne, Peter: *Spitfire on My Tail: A View from the Other Side* (Independent Books, 1989)

Stokes, Doug: *Wings Aflame: The Biography of Group Captain Victor Beamish* (Crecy, 1998)

Taylor, Fred (Editor): *The Goebbels Diaries 1939–41* (Hamish Hamilton, 1982)

Terraine, John: *The Right of the Line: The Royal Air Force in the European War 1939–1945* (Sceptre, 1988)

Townshend Bickers, Richard: *The Battle of Britain* (Salamander, 1990)

The Battle of Britain, August–October 1940. An Air Ministry Account of the Great Days from 8th August to 31st October 1940 (HMSO, 1941)

Thetford, Owen: *Aircraft of the Royal Air Force since 1918* (Putnam & Company, 1979)

We Speak from the Air: Broadcasts by the RAF (HMSO, 1942)

Wellum, Geoffrey: *First Light* (Penguin, 2003)

Williamson, Gordon: *Knight's Cross with Diamonds Recipients: 1941–45* (Osprey, 2012)

Wood, Derek & Dempster, Derek: *The Narrow Margin: The Battle of Britain and the Rise of Air Power, 1930–40* (Hutchinson, 1961)

Zimmerman, David: *Britain's Shield: Radar and the Defeat of the Luftwaffe* (Amberley, 2012)

OTHER SOURCES

The Times

Flight magazine

Ascherson, Neal: 'How phantom German fighter tricked Britain', *The Observer*, 22 October 2000

Despatch from Air Chief Marshal Hugh Dowding to Secretary of State for Air on 20 August 1941, printed in *Supplement to the London Gazette*, 11 September 1946

WEBSITES

Rolls-Royce:
www.rolls-royce.com

The Battle of Britain London Monument:
www.bbm.org.uk

Battle of Britain Historical Society:
www.battleofbritain1940.net

Battle of Britain Memorial Trust:
www.battleofbritainmemorial.org/the-battle-of-britain/the-few

KentOnline:
www.kentonline.co.uk

The Luftwaffe 1933–1945:
www.ww2.dk

New Zealand History Online:
www.nzhistory.net.nz/media/photo/archibald-mcindoe

WWII Aircraft Performance:
www.wwiiaircraftperformance.org

East Anglia Daily Times:
www.eadt.co.uk

TV & Radio

Fighting the Blue (ASA Productions, 2005)

The Heroes of Biggin Hill (Epiphany Productions for Yesterday, 2010)

Now It Can Be Told, BBC Home Service radio programme, 22 May 1945

Timewatch: Operation Sea Lion (BBC, 1998)

I Was There: Battle of Britain documentary (Revelation Films, 2000)

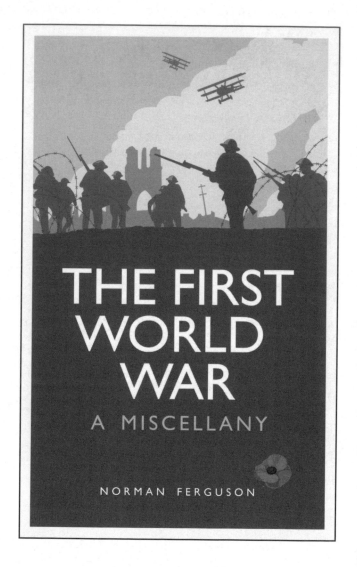

THE FIRST
WORLD
WAR

A MISCELLANY

NORMAN FERGUSON

THE FIRST WORLD WAR

A Miscellany

Norman Ferguson

£9.99

Hardback

ISBN: 978-1-84953-452-9

Have you ever wondered...

- Who fired the first British shot of the First World War?
- Who claimed the glory of downing the Red Baron?
- Who was the first WW1 soldier to receive the Victoria Cross?

Telling the stories of the battles, the aircraft, the weapons, the soldiers, the poets, the campaigns and the many heroes, this comprehensive miscellany is a compelling guide to a war that transformed and marked forever the course of twentieth-century history.

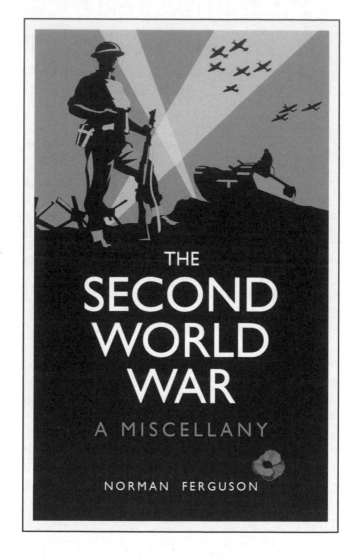

THE
SECOND
WORLD
WAR

A MISCELLANY

NORMAN FERGUSON

THE SECOND WORLD WAR

A Miscellany

Norman Ferguson

£9.99

Hardback

ISBN: 978-1-84953-550-2

Have you ever wondered...

- Who was the deadliest sniper of the war?
- How low did the Dambusters fly?
- How many ships were sunk at Pearl Harbor?

Telling the stories of the Battle of Britain, the Siege of Leningrad, the horrors of the Holocaust, the D-Day landings and the other battles, campaigns, aircraft, weapons, soldiers and heroes on the Home Front and abroad, this is a compelling guide to one of the most destructive and all-encompassing wars the world has ever seen.

Have you enjoyed this book?
If so, why not write a review on your
favourite website?

If you're interested in finding out more about our
books, find us on Facebook at **Summersdale Publishers**
and follow us on Twitter at **@Summersdale**.

Thanks very much for buying this Summersdale book.

www.summersdale.com